The 24-Hour Thriller with ChatGPT

Andrew Parry

Published by Andrew Parry, 2025.

THE 24-HOUR THRILLER WITH CHATGPT

First edition. April 4, 2025.

ISBN: 979-8230404712

Written by Andrew Parry.

Table of Contents

What Makes a Thriller Thrilling?

Before you sit down with ChatGPT to write your thriller in one day, you need to understand what makes a thriller story so gripping, so page-turning, and why readers keep coming back to this genre. If you don't understand the DNA of a thriller, your story will end up flat and mechanical, no matter how fast you write it. So let's break it down and talk about the key ingredients that make a thriller genuinely thrilling.

At its heart, a thriller is a story built on tension. Every chapter, every scene, every line is designed to pull the reader forward, to make them lean in, not back. A good thriller never lets you relax. It doesn't give you the space to breathe easily. There's always a question hanging in the air: what's going to happen next? And better yet, is the protagonist going to survive it?

Thrillers aren't about the characters sitting around thinking about their feelings for long stretches. Sure, character development matters—we'll talk about that in later chapters—but thrillers are about momentum, danger, and uncertainty. Your reader should feel like they're holding their breath the whole way through.

The most basic thing that makes a thriller thrilling is the **presence of a clear threat**. That threat can take many forms. It can be a murderer, a government conspiracy, a bomb that's about to go off, a kidnapping, or even a psychological threat that exists only inside the protagonist's mind. But the point is: there's always something dangerous looming over the characters, and it's urgent. It's a ticking clock, whether literally or metaphorically.

In many other genres, the plot can meander and explore subplots without losing the reader. In thrillers, every subplot should tie back to that main threat. Every side character should either help or hinder the protagonist's attempt to stop whatever bad thing is about to happen. That's what keeps the story tight, clean, and razor-sharp.

Another reason thrillers work is because they play on **fear and uncertainty**. People read thrillers because they want to feel something intense and visceral without actually being in danger themselves. It's a safe way to experience the worst-case scenario. A good thriller will push readers to imagine: What would I do in this situation? Would I survive? Would I make the right choices? That emotional engagement is the hook that keeps them flipping pages at two in the morning.

But it's not just about the action. A thriller without smart plotting and careful manipulation of information will fall flat. A huge part of the thrill is the constant feeling that you, the reader, don't know everything. You're being fed bits of information, clues, and red herrings. You're guessing and second-guessing, wondering who's telling the truth and who's lying. The best thrillers make the reader feel clever one moment and completely blindsided the next.

That's where suspense and misdirection come in. Suspense is all about what the reader knows—or thinks they know. Sometimes, it's about letting the reader in on a secret that the protagonist doesn't know yet, creating tension as the reader waits for the character to catch up. Other times, it's about hiding the truth from everyone and revealing it in a gut-punch twist at just the right moment. You want your readers to be suspicious, anxious, and desperate to figure out the puzzle before it's too late.

The pacing of a thriller is another key element that makes it thrilling. A thriller story is like a rollercoaster—it starts with a climb, builds tension, then plunges into action, only to climb again for the next drop. You want to keep that rhythm going throughout the story. Even in the quieter moments, there should be tension simmering under the surface.

A conversation over coffee isn't just a conversation; it's a strategic exchange of information, a chess game between characters, or a moment of calm before everything explodes.

Good thrillers also tap into **universal fears and anxieties**. Whether it's the fear of being hunted, betrayed, framed, or manipulated, thrillers touch something primal in all of us. That's why the genre is so broad and popular—it speaks to human survival instincts. You can write a thriller about a serial killer, a terrorist attack, a missing child, corporate espionage, a stalker, or even a haunting, and they'll all belong in the same family because they all leverage fear and danger.

Another important aspect of what makes a thriller thrilling is the idea of stakes. If the protagonist fails, something terrible will happen—and not just to them. Maybe the city will be blown up. Maybe someone they love will die. Maybe the world will be changed forever. The stakes are often bigger than the character, and that's why readers care. It's not just personal, it's global or systemic. Even if the story feels small and intimate, the consequences should feel massive to the protagonist.

And let's not forget about the characters. Readers don't come to thrillers for literary prose—they come for the ride. But that doesn't mean you can skimp on your protagonist. Readers want someone they can root for, someone flawed but determined, someone who's being pushed to their limits and still finds a way to keep going. That's what keeps the human element in the middle of all the chaos. You can have the best plot twist in the world, but if your protagonist is dull or unbelievable, no one will care.

The same goes for your antagonist. In a thriller, the villain or threat is just as important as the hero. Sometimes, it's a person. Sometimes, it's an organization. Sometimes, it's even nature itself. But whatever it is, it needs to feel smart, cunning, and one step ahead of the protagonist at every turn. Readers love to see a hero up against something that feels unstoppable—and then watch them find a way to stop it.

So, to sum it up: what makes a thriller thrilling is the **relentless tension, the constant sense of danger, the careful plotting of clues and misdirection, the high stakes, the flawed but determined characters, and the pacing that doesn't let readers put the book down**.

When you understand these things, writing a thriller in one day isn't just possible—it's exciting. Because once you know how to build that tension, how to structure your story so that it ramps up the stakes every chapter, and how to create characters your readers will cheer for and fear, you'll see how easy it is to get ChatGPT to help you do the heavy lifting.

By the end of this book, you'll know exactly how to use this knowledge and apply it inside the ChatGPT interface, feeding it what it needs to give you a killer thriller story in just one day. You're not writing literary fiction here. You're crafting a reading experience—an adrenaline-fueled ride that leaves people breathless.

And that starts with knowing how to thrill your reader.

Why You Can Write a Thriller in One Day

If you've never written a thriller—or any story—in a single day, you're probably skeptical right now. Maybe you're even laughing a little. A whole thriller story in one day? That's impossible, right? But here's the truth: not only is it possible, it's also fun, productive, and entirely doable when you've got ChatGPT as your writing partner and a solid method to follow.

The big myth out there is that writing a thriller has to take months or years. People imagine thriller authors locked away in their offices, drinking black coffee at midnight, agonizing over every sentence. But that's not the only way to do it. What you need to realize is that the long, painful writing process is mostly about hesitation, procrastination, perfectionism, and the belief that a story has to be written slowly to be good. That belief is wrong.

When you break it down, writing a thriller—or any story—is a process of making decisions. You're choosing characters, deciding what happens next, figuring out where to set the scenes, and deciding how to end it. What slows most writers down isn't the typing. It's the endless second-guessing. It's the overthinking. It's the fear of getting it wrong. But with the right strategy, you can eliminate all of that.

This is where ChatGPT changes the game. Think of ChatGPT as a supercharged brainstorming partner who never runs out of energy. The magic isn't just in getting ChatGPT to write text for you—it's about how you can use it to map, structure, and flesh out your entire story in real-time. You're no longer stuck staring at a blank page or wondering what happens next. You're in control, steering the creative process, while ChatGPT helps you fill in the blanks fast.

The reason you can write a thriller in one day is because you can now skip the two things that usually slow writers down: planning paralysis and creative fatigue. You don't have to spend weeks outlining your plot, designing your characters, and figuring out the perfect twist. You can do all of that in hours, collaborating with an AI that can instantly suggest plot points, character flaws, locations, conflicts, and resolutions. You'll still need to make the creative decisions—this is your story, after all—but the heavy lifting of typing, organizing, and refining can happen at lightning speed.

Another reason this is doable is because thrillers follow a very clear structure. There's a formula, whether authors like to admit it or not. You've got a protagonist, an antagonist, a threat, a series of escalating events, and a resolution where everything either falls apart or comes together. That doesn't make thrillers predictable; it makes them efficient to write. Once you understand the building blocks—and we'll cover all of them in this book—you can use them like Lego bricks to assemble your story quickly.

Most thrillers also follow the three-act structure. You start with the setup, introduce the threat, and put your protagonist in the middle of it. Then, you hit them with obstacles and twists that raise the stakes and tension. Finally, you bring everything crashing together in an explosive climax and a satisfying resolution. It's like a recipe. If you follow it, you can bake the cake in a single day, especially when you've got a kitchen assistant like ChatGPT chopping the vegetables and preheating the oven for you.

Writing a thriller in one day isn't about perfection. It's about completion. You're writing a full first draft, not a polished masterpiece. You can always come back later to fine-tune your language, fix plot holes, and clean up dialogue. But the hardest part of writing—the storytelling itself—can absolutely be done in a day, because it's about putting all the pieces on the board quickly and confidently.

One of the best things about using ChatGPT to write your thriller in one day is that you're never writing alone. You're constantly bouncing ideas back and forth. You can say, "Give me five possible twists for this scene," and instantly get options. You can say, "Describe a tense confrontation between my protagonist and their nemesis," and watch the words flow. It removes the burden of filling the blank page on your own and turns the process into a fast-paced, interactive experience.

There's another reason this approach works: momentum. Writing a thriller in one day keeps you inside the story world. You're not stepping away for days or weeks between writing sessions and losing track of the plot. You're riding the wave of the story's tension all the way to the end. That energy translates onto the page. Readers can feel when a story was written with urgency, and thrillers thrive on that sense of movement.

Plus, writing your thriller in one day forces you to trust your instincts. There's no time to overthink or second-guess. You have to make decisions quickly, which often leads to more honest, raw storytelling. Sometimes, your gut will take the story in directions you didn't expect, and that spontaneity is part of what makes thrillers exciting.

You might be wondering if this means the story will be rushed or shallow. Not if you do it right. When you use ChatGPT as a writing assistant, you can still build complex characters, layered plots, and meaningful themes. You'll just be doing it quickly and efficiently, without getting bogged down in analysis paralysis.

Think of it like this: writing a thriller in one day is a creative sprint, not a marathon. You're focused, energized, and committed to reaching the finish line. When you combine that energy with the right tools and a clear method, the result can be astonishing.

Of course, you'll still need to prepare. That's what this book is here for. Over the next chapters, I'll walk you through how to generate ideas quickly, structure your plot in advance, build compelling characters, and manage pacing—all while using ChatGPT to speed up the process without losing creative control.

By the time you're done with this book, you'll have a step-by-step system you can follow any time you want to knock out a thriller story in a single day. You'll be able to sit down at your computer in the morning with nothing but an idea and stand up at night with a finished first draft ready for editing, publishing, or even turning into a screenplay.

So, why can you write a thriller in one day? Because the technology now exists to remove all the obstacles. Because thrillers are built on structure, tension, and high-stakes plotting—all of which can be rapidly mapped and written when you have the right approach. And most importantly, because the story you want to tell is already in your head. You just need a method to get it out fast.

If you've ever dreamed of writing a thriller but thought you didn't have the time, that excuse ends here. You do have the time. You can do it in one day. And by the time you finish this book, you'll know exactly how.

How ChatGPT Becomes Your Co-Writer

By now, you might be wondering how ChatGPT actually fits into the process of writing your thriller story in one day. You know you can do it fast. You know thrillers rely on structure, tension, and pacing. But where does ChatGPT come in? Is it just another tool? Is it going to write the story for you? Or is it something more?

Here's the answer: ChatGPT is your co-writer. Not your ghostwriter. Not your replacement. Your co-writer. And when you learn how to use it right, it becomes the most efficient, supportive, and tireless writing partner you'll ever have.

A lot of people think AI writing tools like ChatGPT are about pressing a button and getting a finished story. That's not how it works, and honestly, that's not what you want. The soul of your story—the creative spark, the originality, the twists, the characters—that still has to come from you. ChatGPT isn't here to create for you. It's here to create with you.

Think of ChatGPT like a hyper-intelligent writing assistant who never gets tired, never complains, and can brainstorm with you at the speed of thought. It's like having a room full of writing interns who will instantly write whatever you ask, pitch you twenty plot twists on demand, or help you shape a complex character in minutes.

The beauty of using ChatGPT is that it can help you overcome the biggest obstacle to writing: the blank page. When you sit down to write a thriller, the hardest part is often knowing where to start. ChatGPT removes that problem completely. You can tell it, "Give me ten unique thriller story ideas," and you'll have them in seconds. You can ask, "Describe a thrilling opening scene involving a hostage situation in a skyscraper," and boom—it's there on the screen.

But that's just the beginning. The real power of ChatGPT is in the collaboration. You can shape and reshape your story interactively, asking for rewrites, more options, alternative dialogue, or even scene summaries. You can treat it like a writing room, bouncing ideas back and forth, seeing what sticks, and refining your plot in real time.

Let's say you want to write a psychological thriller about a detective who starts to suspect he's the criminal he's hunting. You can feed that concept into ChatGPT and instantly start building out the details. You can ask it to help you structure the three acts. You can brainstorm the detective's backstory, create a list of red herrings, develop side characters, or even ask for examples of tense dialogue between the detective and the suspect. ChatGPT will give you options, and you choose what works best for your story.

One of the best ways to use ChatGPT as your co-writer is by treating it like a conversation, not a vending machine. The more you engage, refine, and steer the AI, the better your results will be. It's not about typing "Write me a thriller story" and hitting send. It's about having an ongoing, creative dialogue. You give ChatGPT direction, it gives you material, and you shape that material into the story you want to tell.

Another thing that makes ChatGPT such a great co-writer is that it's completely ego-free. You can ask it for five different versions of the same scene without worrying about offending it. You can reject everything it writes without hurting anyone's feelings. That creative freedom is priceless because it allows you to experiment, make mistakes, and keep pushing the story forward without any emotional baggage slowing you down.

It's also worth mentioning that ChatGPT never suffers from writer's block. You can always ask it to keep going, suggest a new idea, or fill in the next scene. Even when you're stuck, it isn't. That means you can keep your momentum going without getting bogged down in creative frustration.

But here's the key to making ChatGPT a truly effective co-writer: you have to stay in control. The AI can generate text, ideas, characters, and dialogue, but you're the one who has to decide what fits your story. It's easy to get lazy and start copy-pasting everything it writes without thinking critically, but that's not how you create a gripping thriller. You need to use ChatGPT as a tool, not a crutch.

When you're writing your thriller in one day, you're essentially running a writing sprint. You don't have time to waste, but you also can't afford to lose creative control. ChatGPT helps you by handling the grunt work—filling in descriptions, suggesting dialogue, outlining scenes—so you can focus on the bigger creative decisions: the twists, the stakes, the pacing, and the overall vision.

One of the best strategies is to use ChatGPT in stages. Start by brainstorming and outlining. Get it to help you map out the entire story structure quickly. Once you know your plot, use ChatGPT to flesh out the characters. Then, when you start writing, you can use it to draft scenes, polish dialogue, and even help you fix pacing issues on the fly. This staged approach keeps you in the driver's seat while letting the AI handle the heavy lifting.

You can also use ChatGPT to generate multiple versions of the same scene and then combine the best parts. For example, if you're writing a scene where your protagonist breaks into a secure facility, you can ask ChatGPT to write three different versions of that scene with varying tension and detail. Then you can pick the parts you like, rewrite others, and stitch them together into something that feels fresh and uniquely yours.

Another huge advantage of working with ChatGPT is speed. You'll be amazed at how fast you can move when you're not writing every sentence yourself. You'll go from a blank page to a finished draft in a matter of hours because you're not getting stuck on small details. ChatGPT can handle those details while you keep your eyes on the bigger picture.

There's one more thing you need to understand about using ChatGPT as your co-writer: it's only as good as the prompts you give it. The clearer, more specific, and more creative your prompts are, the better the AI's output will be. That's why this book will also teach you how to write killer prompts that get ChatGPT to produce exactly what you need, fast.

By the time you've worked your way through this process, you'll realize something powerful: you're not just using ChatGPT to write faster—you're learning how to think like a thriller writer. You'll start recognizing plot structures, character arcs, pacing tricks, and suspense techniques without even thinking about them. ChatGPT will help you build those muscles quickly and effortlessly.

So, to sum it up, ChatGPT becomes your co-writer by being your brainstorming partner, your scene generator, your dialogue assistant, and your pacing consultant—all rolled into one. But you're still the storyteller. You're still the creative force behind the narrative. ChatGPT is the tool that lets you tell that story faster, smarter, and with less stress.

The Importance of Story Concept in Thrillers

If you want to write a thriller in one day, you've got to understand this: it all starts with the concept. Without a strong, clear, thrilling concept, no amount of cool characters, shocking twists, or fast-paced scenes will save your story. The concept is the engine that drives everything else. It's the hook that grabs the reader by the throat and says, "You need to read this."

A weak concept leads to a weak thriller. It's that simple. That's why, before you start typing, before you even outline, you need to nail the idea. And luckily, with ChatGPT as your co-writer, you can brainstorm and refine your concept in minutes.

So what exactly is a concept? It's not just an idea—it's the central premise of your story, the thing that makes people want to know more. It's the "what if" at the heart of your thriller. What if a woman wakes up with no memory, and the man claiming to be her husband isn't who he says he is? What if a detective's family is being held hostage unless he sabotages his own investigation? What if a journalist uncovers a global conspiracy but is being hunted before she can reveal the truth?

These are story concepts. They're clear, gripping, and packed with conflict. And in the thriller genre, they almost always have three things in common: high stakes, tension, and danger.

High stakes mean that something important is on the line. It could be the protagonist's life, someone they love, their reputation, or even the fate of the entire world. The reader needs to feel that if the protagonist fails, something terrible will happen.

Tension is all about uncertainty. A good concept sets up a situation where the outcome is unknown and the reader has to keep turning pages to find out what happens.

Danger is what makes a thriller a thriller. Whether it's physical danger, psychological manipulation, or a looming catastrophe, your concept has to threaten the protagonist in a real, visceral way.

When you start writing with ChatGPT, one of the first things you should do is workshop your concept. Don't just settle for the first idea that pops into your head. Push it further. Make it sharper. Ask ChatGPT for variations. Play with the stakes, the danger, the protagonist's predicament. Keep going until you've got a concept that makes your heart race—because if it doesn't excite you, it won't excite your readers.

Here's how you can use ChatGPT to nail your concept. Start with a simple prompt like, "Give me ten high-stakes thriller story concepts." You'll get a list of raw ideas. Some will be cliché. Some will be too far-fetched. Some will be close but not quite right. That's fine. Your job is to sift through them, pick one that sparks something, and then refine it.

Once you've picked a concept you like, don't stop there. Dig deeper. Ask ChatGPT to expand the idea. Ask it to raise the stakes. Ask it to twist the premise in unexpected ways. You can even ask it to blend two different concepts together to create something fresh. The more you play with the idea, the more original and gripping it becomes.

Let's say your concept is: "A detective races to catch a serial killer who leaves cryptic messages at every crime scene." That's fine, but it's been done. How do you make it yours? Maybe you ask ChatGPT to flip the concept. What if the detective realizes the messages are directed at him? What if the killer is someone he knows? What if catching the killer means sacrificing someone he loves?

The concept is also where you start planting the seeds of your plot twists. A good thriller concept contains the possibility of surprise. It's not just a straightforward chase. There's something underneath, something readers won't see coming. Your concept should make the reader wonder, "How is this going to end?"

Another reason the concept is so important is because it keeps you focused. When you're writing a thriller in one day, you don't have time to wander off course. A clear, powerful concept gives you a roadmap. Every scene, every character, every twist should tie back to that central premise. If it doesn't, it doesn't belong in your story.

Think of your concept as the spine of your thriller. The plot, characters, setting, and pacing—all of that hangs off the spine. If the spine is weak, the story collapses. If it's strong, everything else will hold together no matter how fast you're writing.

Your concept also helps you decide what kind of thriller you're writing. Is it a psychological thriller, where the real danger is inside the protagonist's mind? Is it an action-packed international thriller with car chases and shootouts? Is it a domestic thriller about secrets and lies in a marriage? The concept shapes the tone, the setting, and the kind of tension you're going to build.

And let's not forget the marketing angle. If you plan to publish and sell your thriller story, the concept is what will grab readers when they see your book cover or read the description. People don't buy thrillers because of the writing style. They buy them because the concept makes them want to know what happens next.

The good news is that you don't have to agonize over your concept for days. ChatGPT can help you brainstorm, refine, and sharpen it quickly. But you do need to spend the time up front to make sure your concept is solid. It's tempting to rush past this step and dive into writing, but if you skip the concept stage, you'll waste time later when your plot starts to fall apart.

So before you write a single scene, sit down with ChatGPT and develop your concept. Ask it for ideas. Push the boundaries. Challenge the AI to come up with something you haven't seen before. Test the concept by imagining the ending. If you can already picture a jaw-dropping climax, you're on the right track.

A great thriller doesn't start with clever sentences or flashy action scenes. It starts with a razor-sharp concept that demands to be told. That's what hooks readers. That's what keeps them turning pages. And that's what will carry you through the process of writing an entire thriller story in a single day.

In the next chapter, we'll dig into exactly how to generate those killer thriller ideas quickly and efficiently—so you're never stuck wondering what story to tell.

Generating Killer Thriller Ideas with ChatGPT

So you're sitting at your desk, coffee in hand, ready to write a thriller in one day. But before you can start typing, you need an idea. Not just any idea—a killer idea. An idea that grips you by the throat and won't let go. This is where a lot of writers stumble. They waste hours staring at a blank page, waiting for inspiration to strike. But when you've got ChatGPT in your corner, you don't need to wait for the muse. You can summon it on demand.

One of the biggest advantages of using ChatGPT is how quickly it can help you generate fresh, exciting thriller ideas. You don't have to sit there alone, brainstorming until your brain hurts. You can have an entire list of potential stories in front of you in seconds. And the more you engage with the AI, the better the ideas will get.

The process is simple, but powerful. You start with a basic prompt. Something like, "Give me ten unique thriller story ideas." ChatGPT will give you a list. Some will be cliché. Some will feel generic. But usually, at least one or two will spark something in your imagination. That's all you need to get started.

But don't stop there. Once you've got a spark, it's time to fan the flames. You can ask ChatGPT to expand on that idea. Let's say one of the ideas is, "A detective wakes up in a foreign country with no memory and is framed for a crime he didn't commit." That's a solid start, but you want to make it yours. So you ask ChatGPT, "Tell me more about this detective. What crime is he accused of? Who framed him? What's the twist?" In seconds, you'll get answers that help you shape the core of your story.

You can keep pushing. Ask for three different versions of the idea. Ask how the story could end. Ask for ways to raise the stakes. ChatGPT will keep feeding you possibilities until you find the one that makes your pulse race.

One of the best techniques for idea generation is blending. You can feed ChatGPT two different concepts and ask it to combine them into something new. For example, you might say, "Mix a political thriller with a psychological thriller. Give me three story ideas." The results will often surprise you and take you in directions you never would've thought of on your own.

You can also reverse-engineer ideas. Start by asking ChatGPT for thrilling endings. Something like, "Give me five shocking endings for a thriller story." Then, once you've got an ending that excites you, work backward. Ask, "What kind of story would lead to this ending?" This approach is one of the most powerful ways to generate tight, focused thrillers because you're starting with the payoff and building toward it.

Another trick is to focus on the kind of protagonist or villain you want. You can ask ChatGPT, "Give me ten ideas for thrillers with a female protagonist who has a dark secret." Or, "Give me thriller story ideas where the villain is someone the hero loves." The more specific your prompt, the better the ideas will be. And the more tailored they'll be to the kind of story you want to write.

Don't be afraid to throw wild prompts at ChatGPT. Sometimes the best ideas come from the weirdest combinations. You might say, "Give me a thriller story idea involving a detective, a missing painting, and a doomsday cult." The AI will pull something together, and even if it's messy, you'll often find a seed of brilliance hiding in the middle of the chaos.

Remember, idea generation is a numbers game. The more ideas you get, the better your chances of finding one that sticks. ChatGPT makes it easy to generate dozens of concepts in a short amount of time. You're no longer limited by your own brainpower or creativity. You can keep going until you find an idea that makes you want to drop everything and start writing.

Once you've found your core idea, use ChatGPT to start fleshing it out immediately. Ask for a one-paragraph summary of the story. Then a three-act structure. Then a list of key characters. Then possible plot twists. You'll be amazed at how quickly your story starts to take shape.

But here's the thing: don't settle for the first draft of the idea. Use ChatGPT to refine it. Challenge it. Push it to make the concept sharper, the stakes higher, the twists more unexpected. Keep asking, "How can I make this more thrilling?" until you've got a concept that feels like it could sit on a bookstore shelf next to the bestsellers.

Also, trust your instincts. You're the storyteller. ChatGPT will throw a lot of ideas at you, but you have to choose the one that excites you the most. The one you can't stop thinking about. That's the story you're going to write in one day.

The last thing to remember is that your idea doesn't have to be perfect. You're going to shape and refine it as you write. What matters is that it has a clear threat, high stakes, and the potential for tension and twists. If you've got that, you've got enough to start.

Idea generation isn't a mystical process. It's practical, fast, and efficient when you've got the right tools—and ChatGPT is the best tool you've got. By the time you finish this chapter, you should have at least one thriller concept that makes your heart race. That's your green light to move on to the next step: turning that idea into a structured plot you can write in a day.

In the next chapter, we're going to talk about how to reverse-engineer your story and build it from the ending backward. That's where the real magic starts, and it's how you'll make sure your thriller is tight, thrilling, and satisfying from start to finish.

Starting with the End: The Thriller Finale

One of the fastest, smartest ways to write a thriller story in one day is to start where most writers end—at the finale. That might sound backward, but trust me, this approach will save you time, give you focus, and guarantee that your thriller is tight, thrilling, and actually works. It's also the reason so many bestselling thriller authors swear by reverse-engineering their stories.

Here's why: The ending of a thriller isn't just another scene. It's the entire point. It's the payoff, the reason the reader stuck with you through all the twists, tension, and chaos. If your ending is weak, the entire story collapses. But when your ending is strong, everything else can be built to serve that moment. That's why we start there.

Think of it like building a house. You wouldn't start randomly putting up walls and windows without knowing where the front door is going to be. Same with a thriller story. You start by asking: How does this story end? What is the final twist, the last confrontation, the big reveal, or the final victory or loss?

This is especially important when you're writing fast. If you know exactly where you're going, you'll never waste time wondering what happens next. Every scene you write will be a step toward that ending. That's why this chapter is all about designing your finale before you write anything else.

A great thriller ending has a few key elements. First, it has **impact**. It's not just the resolution of the plot; it's an emotional punch. It leaves the reader breathless, stunned, satisfied, or shaken. It's the moment when the final puzzle piece clicks into place and everything makes sense—or everything falls apart.

Second, a great ending has **surprise**. This doesn't mean it has to be a twist ending, but there should be something unexpected. Maybe the protagonist wins, but at a terrible cost. Maybe the villain was someone they trusted all along. Maybe the protagonist realizes they've been manipulated the entire time. Whatever it is, the ending should deliver something the reader didn't fully see coming—but something that, once revealed, feels inevitable.

Third, a strong thriller ending has **closure**. The questions raised by the story are answered. The loose ends are tied up. The reader isn't left wondering what happened. That doesn't mean everything has to be happy or neatly resolved, but the story has to feel complete.

So how do you use ChatGPT to design your thriller ending quickly and effectively?

Start by telling ChatGPT the basic concept you've developed. For example, "I'm writing a thriller about a detective who's framed for murder by his former partner." Then ask, "Give me five possible endings for this story, each with a shocking twist."

In seconds, you'll get a list of options. Some might be predictable. Some might be wild. Some might spark an idea you hadn't considered. That's the magic. You can then say, "I like ending number three. Expand on that. Show me how it could unfold in the final scene." ChatGPT will give you a detailed draft of your finale.

You can keep refining. Ask for more danger, more emotional impact, or more surprise. Tell ChatGPT to give you variations. Combine different endings. Shape the climax into something you love. You're not settling for the first version—you're sculpting the ending you want.

Another trick is to work backward from your chosen ending. Once you know how the story ends, you can start asking, "What needs to happen in Act Two to lead to this ending? What obstacles should the protagonist face? What lies or red herrings can I plant earlier in the story?" ChatGPT can help you map the whole thing out in minutes.

For example, if your ending involves the protagonist discovering that their closest ally is the real villain, you can work backward and ask, "How can I plant clues about this ally's betrayal without giving it away too soon?" ChatGPT will suggest scenes, dialogue hints, and character behavior you can weave into the story.

The beauty of starting with the end is that it keeps your thriller focused. You're no longer wandering in the dark, making up scenes and hoping it all comes together. You're building toward something specific, and that makes your writing faster and more intentional.

Another benefit is that it keeps the pacing tight. You'll know exactly how much ground you need to cover and how quickly you need to escalate the tension to reach that ending. It's like having a map with the destination circled in red. You might take a few detours along the way, but you're always moving toward that final confrontation.

It also helps you stay motivated. Writing a full thriller story in one day can feel like a marathon, but when you know exactly where you're headed, you're less likely to get stuck. You can focus on making each scene build toward that explosive climax, rather than wasting time wondering what's supposed to happen next.

When you're developing your ending, make sure you also think about your protagonist's journey. What has changed for them by the end? Have they won or lost? Have they grown stronger, or been broken by the experience? Thrillers aren't just about plot—they're about how the characters are transformed by the danger they face.

Use ChatGPT to help you map out your protagonist's emotional arc. Ask, "How does the protagonist change by the end of this story?" or "What emotional payoff can I give readers in the final scene?" The AI can help you shape not just the plot but the heart of your thriller.

One final tip: when you're writing your ending with ChatGPT, don't be afraid to go big. This is the moment your entire story is building toward. Make it intense. Make it shocking. Make it unforgettable. Whether it's a last-minute betrayal, a deadly confrontation, or a gut-wrenching sacrifice, your ending is what readers will remember.

And because you're working with ChatGPT, you can draft multiple versions of the finale quickly and choose the one that hits hardest. You can even combine the best parts of each version into a single, powerful conclusion.

So don't wait until the end of your writing day to figure out how your thriller ends. Start with the ending. Design it. Refine it. Make it bulletproof. Then, when you start writing, you'll be racing toward that finish line with purpose and clarity.

In the next chapter, we'll dive into how to reverse-engineer your entire thriller plot based on the ending you've just created—so you can outline and structure your story in record time.

Reverse Engineering Your Thriller Plot

Now that you've got your killer ending locked in, it's time to do something most writers never think of doing—but something that will make writing your thriller in one day not only possible but actually enjoyable. It's time to reverse-engineer your entire plot. You're going to work backwards, building the trail of tension, danger, and twists that lead straight to that jaw-dropping finale you've already created.

This method isn't new. A lot of professional screenwriters, novelists, and filmmakers use this approach without shouting about it. Why? Because it works. Especially in the thriller genre, where pacing, plotting, and setups that pay off in shocking ways are everything. When you start at the end, you know exactly what you need to plant in the beginning and middle to make that ending hit hard.

Let's break down how this works in practice. You've already designed your ending—maybe it's a dramatic rooftop showdown where your protagonist finally confronts the person who's been manipulating them all along. That's your destination. Now you need to build the path that gets them there.

First, look at the climax and ask yourself a simple question: **What does the reader need to know and feel in order for this ending to matter?** That's the heart of reverse engineering. You're going to figure out which information, clues, relationships, and conflicts need to be introduced earlier in the story to make your ending feel inevitable yet surprising.

For example, if your ending involves the protagonist realizing that their trusted friend is the real villain, you need to plant signs of that betrayal in the first and second acts. Maybe it's subtle moments of manipulation. Maybe it's small lies that don't seem important at first. Maybe it's tension in the friend's backstory. When you reverse-engineer your plot, you'll start looking for ways to lace those details into your story from the very first chapter.

This process also helps you avoid one of the biggest mistakes new thriller writers make: adding twists that feel cheap or random. A good twist isn't about shocking readers for the sake of it—it's about revealing something that was hiding in plain sight all along. Reverse engineering ensures that your twists are earned because you've built the groundwork from the start.

You can use ChatGPT to make this process ridiculously fast. Start by telling it your ending. For example: "My thriller ends with Detective Sarah confronting her former partner, who's been the killer all along." Then ask, "What clues and events should I include in Acts One and Two to lead to this ending without giving it away too early?" ChatGPT will instantly give you a list of ideas—maybe moments of misdirection, suspicious behavior, red herrings, and key discoveries.

From there, you can start mapping out the major plot points backward. Think of it like connecting the dots in reverse. Your ending is Dot #10. What's Dot #9—the scene right before the climax? Maybe it's when Sarah finally pieces together the clues. What's Dot #8—the scene before that? Maybe it's when she finds a piece of evidence she'd overlooked. You keep working backward until you reach the start of the story.

You can literally ask ChatGPT to do this for you. Give it your ending and say, "Map out ten key plot points in reverse order that lead to this ending." Boom—you'll have a rough outline in minutes.

The other reason reverse engineering is so effective is because it keeps your plot tight. When you're writing a thriller in one day, you don't have time for scenes that go nowhere. You don't want your reader slogging through filler chapters. Every scene should either escalate the tension, reveal new information, deepen the conflict, or bring the protagonist closer to (or further from) their goal. When you plot backwards, you can see exactly which scenes are essential and which ones aren't.

It also helps with pacing. Thriller stories are like rollercoasters. They start with a slow climb, then build speed, tension, and danger until everything explodes at the end. Reverse engineering lets you map out those peaks and valleys in advance. You can see where the big twists need to happen, where to slow things down for a quiet moment of doubt, and where to crank up the action.

Another benefit is character development. When you know how your protagonist's story ends, you can shape their arc more clearly. You can decide what kind of person they need to be at the beginning—and what experiences will change them by the end. You can also make sure your antagonist's actions make sense and build toward that final confrontation.

Let's say your protagonist starts out as a naïve rookie cop and ends the story as a hardened, disillusioned survivor. You can reverse-engineer the key events that force them to change—the betrayals, the losses, the hard choices they have to make. That way, their arc feels natural and powerful.

You can also use this method to layer in subplots and secondary characters. If you want a subplot about the protagonist's estranged daughter, ask yourself: How does her story connect to the ending? What role does she play in the climax? Then work backward to figure out how to weave her storyline into the main plot without slowing things down.

Here's another practical tip: once you've mapped out your plot backwards, flip it back around and look at the structure from start to finish. Ask ChatGPT to turn your reverse outline into a forward-moving one. That way, when you sit down to write, you'll have a clear, step-by-step roadmap to follow.

Some writers resist this kind of plotting because they think it kills creativity. But the truth is, reverse engineering frees you up to be creative without wasting time. You've already solved the hardest part—the structure. Now, when you're writing, you can focus on making each scene thrilling, intense, and full of personality because you're not worrying about where the story is going.

The final reason this method is so powerful is simple: thrillers are about payoff. Readers want to feel like the ending hits them hard but makes perfect sense. They want to look back and see how all the pieces fit together. When you reverse-engineer your plot, you guarantee that satisfaction because you've built the story from the payoff backward.

In the next chapter, we'll dive deeper into creating a high-stakes protagonist—the heart and soul of your thriller—and how to use ChatGPT to bring them to life in record time.

Creating a High-Stakes Protagonist

You can have the best thriller plot in the world—the coolest twists, the deadliest villains, the most shocking finale—but if your protagonist is dull, flat, or forgettable, your story will collapse like a house of cards. The beating heart of every thriller is the protagonist. It's their journey, their decisions, their desperation, and their survival that keep readers turning pages at two in the morning. So, if you want to write a killer thriller in one day, you need to create a high-stakes protagonist—and you need to do it fast.

Let's start with what I mean by "high-stakes." A high-stakes protagonist isn't just someone who wants something. It's someone who **needs** something desperately, and who has everything to lose if they fail. In a thriller, your protagonist's stakes aren't mild or vague. They're life-or-death, freedom-or-prison, sanity-or-madness, trust-or-betrayal kind of stakes. That's what keeps readers hooked. It's not just about the plot; it's about who's living through it.

When you sit down to write your thriller in a day, you don't have time to labor over building your protagonist's entire life story from scratch. That's where ChatGPT comes in. You can use it to sketch out your protagonist quickly, layer by layer, until you've got someone who feels real, flawed, and compelling.

Start by asking ChatGPT something simple like, "Give me ten thriller protagonist ideas." It'll give you a range of characters—detectives, journalists, spies, innocent bystanders caught in a deadly game. Pick one that grabs your attention. Then, drill down. Ask ChatGPT, "What's this character's biggest fear? What's their dark secret? What's at stake for them if they fail?"

You want to build a protagonist who's not just reacting to the plot but who has personal skin in the game. Maybe they're trying to save their kidnapped daughter. Maybe they're trying to clear their name before they go to prison. Maybe they're chasing the villain because if they don't, they'll lose everything they've worked for. Whatever it is, the stakes should be personal and emotional, not just physical.

A high-stakes protagonist is usually flawed. Nobody wants to read about a perfect hero. Readers want someone who's scared, broken, angry, or conflicted—but who keeps going anyway. The thriller genre thrives on characters who are being pushed to their limits, who make mistakes, who doubt themselves but don't give up.

This is where you can use ChatGPT to develop your protagonist's flaws and strengths fast. Ask, "What are five possible flaws for this character?" or "How does this character's past affect their decisions in the story?" You'll get instant answers you can build on.

Another important part of creating a high-stakes protagonist is giving them a clear motivation. What drives them? What's the one thing they want more than anything else? And what's standing in their way? In a thriller, the protagonist's goal is usually survival, truth, justice, revenge, or protecting someone they love. But the more specific you can make it, the better.

For example, it's not enough to say, "She wants to catch the killer." Why? What's at stake for her personally? Maybe she wants to catch the killer because she was blamed for a similar crime years ago and has been living in the shadow of that accusation ever since. Maybe she needs to prove to herself that she's not a failure. Maybe she's hunting the killer because the next victim is her brother. Specific, personal motivation is what will make readers care.

You can use ChatGPT to help you flesh out this motivation quickly. Ask, "What personal reason could this character have for chasing the villain?" or "What past trauma could make this protagonist obsessed with stopping the crime?"

You also want to make sure your protagonist is active, not passive. They shouldn't just react to events—they should drive the story forward with their decisions, mistakes, and risks. A thriller protagonist is a doer. They're not waiting for someone to save them; they're fighting tooth and nail, even when the odds are against them.

Once you've sketched out your protagonist's personality, flaws, strengths, and motivation, the next step is to make sure their personal arc ties into the main plot. In a great thriller, the external conflict (the villain, the conspiracy, the danger) is always linked to the protagonist's internal conflict. Maybe they have to overcome their fear of failure to stop the threat. Maybe they have to learn to trust someone again. Maybe they have to confront their own dark side.

You can ask ChatGPT to help you connect these dots. Try a prompt like, "How can I link this character's personal journey to the main plot of the thriller?" or "What kind of emotional growth can this protagonist experience by the end of the story?"

Another great trick is to ask ChatGPT for scene ideas that reveal your protagonist's personality under pressure. Thriller readers don't want long monologues about how the character feels. They want to see the character's fear, anger, doubt, and determination through action. You can prompt ChatGPT with, "Give me three tense scenes that show this protagonist's flaws and strengths."

And here's something many writers forget: your protagonist doesn't have to be likable at the start. They don't even have to be heroic. They just have to be interesting. Readers will follow a protagonist who's bitter, broken, or morally gray—as long as they're compelling and the stakes are clear. Sometimes, the more flawed your protagonist, the more thrilling their journey becomes.

One last thing to keep in mind is vulnerability. A high-stakes protagonist is never invincible. If the reader knows they'll always win, there's no tension. Your protagonist needs to fail, suffer, doubt themselves, and make mistakes. The danger has to feel real. That's what makes the stakes matter.

And you can use ChatGPT to inject that vulnerability quickly. Ask, "What's a believable weakness this protagonist has that could cost them everything in the climax?" or "What mistake does the protagonist make in Act Two that almost ruins everything?"

By the time you finish this chapter, you should have a fully developed protagonist with clear goals, personal stakes, flaws, strengths, and an emotional journey that ties into the plot. All of this can be built in less than an hour with ChatGPT guiding the process.

Once you've got your protagonist ready, you're well on your way to writing your thriller story in a single day. In the next chapter, we'll talk about how to build the other half of the equation—the antagonist who will make your protagonist's life a living nightmare.

Building Your Antagonist: The Shadow of Fear

If your protagonist is the heart of your thriller, then the antagonist is the shadow looming over that heart—the force that makes every chapter pulse with tension. A thriller is only as good as its villain, threat, or opposing force. Without a great antagonist, there's no danger, no suspense, and no stakes. Your protagonist needs something—or someone—relentless to go up against, and that's where your antagonist comes in.

It's easy to think of an antagonist as just "the bad guy," but in a thriller, they're much more than that. The antagonist is the architect of tension. They're the one who creates the chaos, the danger, the puzzles, and the obstacles. They're the reason your protagonist can't breathe easy until the final page.

When you're writing a thriller in one day, you don't have time to spend weeks inventing a complex villain. But that's okay, because with ChatGPT as your co-writer, you can design a layered, terrifying antagonist quickly and effectively. You just need to know what makes a great thriller antagonist—and how to use ChatGPT to build one fast.

Let's start with the basics. A great antagonist in a thriller has clear goals, just like your protagonist. They're not evil just for the sake of it. They want something. Power, revenge, control, money, recognition, or sometimes something more twisted—like chaos or destruction. The key is that their goal **directly conflicts** with the protagonist's goal. One cannot succeed without the other failing.

That's the first thing you want to figure out. What does your antagonist want? You can use ChatGPT to help you brainstorm. Try a prompt like, "Give me ten thriller antagonist goals that would create maximum conflict with a protagonist trying to solve a mystery." You'll get a range of ideas, from classic to creative.

Once you've got the goal, the next step is to make the antagonist formidable. Readers don't want a villain who's easy to beat. They want an antagonist who feels **smarter, stronger, and always one step ahead**. Someone who forces the protagonist to push beyond their limits. A great thriller villain is a worthy opponent, not a cardboard cutout.

Ask ChatGPT, "What skills, resources, or connections could make this antagonist nearly unstoppable?" It might be wealth, political power, physical strength, psychological manipulation, insider knowledge, or the ability to hide in plain sight.

Another critical element of a great thriller antagonist is **personal connection**. The best villains aren't random strangers; they're tangled up in the protagonist's life in some way. Maybe they were once friends. Maybe they're family. Maybe they share a dark secret. This personal link raises the stakes and adds emotional weight to the conflict.

You can use ChatGPT to develop this connection fast. Prompt it with, "How can I connect this antagonist to the protagonist's past in a surprising way?" or "What personal history could these two characters share that would create tension and betrayal?"

But a truly memorable antagonist isn't just dangerous. They're also human. Readers love villains with depth. What's driving them? What wound, belief, or desire makes them do what they do? You don't have to justify their actions, but you do want to understand them.

You can ask ChatGPT, "What is this antagonist's backstory? What happened to them to make them dangerous?" This will help you avoid clichés and create a villain who feels real, even if they're terrifying.

Another thing to consider is the antagonist's tactics. How do they operate? Are they a master manipulator who turns friends into enemies? Are they brutal and violent, leaving a trail of bodies behind them? Do they hide in the shadows, pulling strings while the protagonist struggles to figure out what's really going on?

Again, ChatGPT can help. Try a prompt like, "Give me five methods this antagonist uses to stay ahead of the protagonist," or "What strategies could this villain use to manipulate the protagonist throughout the story?"

You also want to think about how your antagonist escalates the tension. A great thriller villain doesn't make one move and then sit back. They keep applying pressure, forcing the protagonist into tighter and tighter corners. Every time the protagonist thinks they've won, the antagonist reveals a new, more dangerous plan.

Ask ChatGPT, "How can this antagonist escalate the conflict at key points in the story?" It will help you design the chess game between hero and villain, so the tension keeps ratcheting up.

And don't forget the **fear factor**. Your antagonist should create dread every time they appear on the page—even if they're not physically present. Their actions, plans, and influence should hang over every scene like a dark cloud. Readers should feel the protagonist's anxiety, always wondering what the antagonist will do next.

You can use ChatGPT to help you build this atmosphere. Prompt it with, "How can I make this antagonist's presence felt even when they're not on the page?" or "What psychological tactics could this villain use to terrify the protagonist?"

Finally, think about the antagonist's endgame. How do they react when the protagonist starts to close in? Do they get desperate and violent? Do they try to manipulate their way out? Do they have a last-ditch plan to destroy everything? A great villain fights until the very end, and their downfall should be as dramatic and impactful as the story itself.

Use ChatGPT to map this out. Ask, "What is this antagonist's final move in the climax of the story?" and "What personal or emotional weakness could lead to their defeat?"

By the time you're done building your antagonist, you should have a character who's smart, dangerous, personally connected to the protagonist, and relentless in their pursuit of their goal. They should feel like a real threat—someone the protagonist must overcome not just physically, but emotionally and mentally.

And remember, ChatGPT is your secret weapon here. You can use it to brainstorm, refine, and deepen your antagonist in a matter of minutes. You're not starting from scratch. You're shaping the pieces until they fit perfectly into your story.

In the next chapter, we'll talk about the supporting characters—the allies, informants, and obstacles who will help or hinder your protagonist as they race toward the climax.

Crafting Supporting Characters with Purpose

When you're writing a thriller story—especially when you're writing it in one day—it's tempting to treat the supporting characters like background furniture. You might think the protagonist and antagonist are the only ones who matter. But the truth is, the supporting characters in your thriller are just as important. They're the ones who populate the world, add layers of tension and emotional weight, and help (or hinder) your protagonist every step of the way.

A great supporting character can turn an average thriller into an unforgettable one. They can be the trusted ally, the mysterious informant, the unreliable witness, the traitorous friend, or the unexpected wildcard who throws everything into chaos. The key is to make sure every supporting character serves a clear purpose in your story.

And when you're trying to write the entire story in one day, you don't have time to waste on pointless characters. You need to craft them quickly and deliberately, and that's exactly where ChatGPT can help.

So, let's break down how you can use supporting characters to strengthen your thriller and how to develop them fast.

First, understand what supporting characters are **for** in a thriller. They're not just there to fill space. They're functional. Each one should either help the protagonist, hinder the protagonist, reveal information, increase the tension, or raise the stakes. If a supporting character isn't doing at least one of these things, they probably don't belong in your story.

Start by thinking about the kind of people your protagonist would naturally interact with during the course of the thriller. If your story is about a detective, you might need a police partner, a chief who doesn't believe them, a forensic analyst, a key witness, or even a journalist who keeps sticking their nose where it doesn't belong. If your story is about an ordinary person caught in a deadly game, they might have a best friend, a sibling, a love interest, or a neighbor who becomes crucial at the worst possible moment.

Once you've got a rough idea, use ChatGPT to speed up the process. Ask, "Give me ten supporting character ideas for a thriller story about [insert your protagonist's situation]." You'll instantly get a list of potential allies, enemies, informants, and obstacles.

But don't stop at generic descriptions. Flesh them out. For each one, ask ChatGPT, "What secret is this character hiding?" or "What personal conflict does this character have with the protagonist?" You want these characters to feel real, with motivations, flaws, and agendas of their own.

One of the best ways to make supporting characters matter is to tie them emotionally to the protagonist. Maybe the protagonist's closest ally is also their ex-lover. Maybe the person giving them information is someone they betrayed years ago. Maybe the person standing in their way is a family member with a grudge. These connections create tension, deepen the stakes, and keep the reader invested.

You can prompt ChatGPT with, "How can I connect this supporting character to the protagonist's past?" or "What personal history could make this ally unreliable or dangerous?"

Another thing to keep in mind is variety. Your supporting characters should feel distinct. You don't want a cast of clones who all serve the same function. Mix it up. Give your protagonist an ally who's all-in and loyal to the end—but also give them a skeptic who doubts their every move. Throw in a wildcard character who seems helpful but might have their own hidden agenda.

Ask ChatGPT, "Give me five supporting character archetypes I can use in this thriller," and you'll get a range of roles to fill.

You should also think about how your supporting characters impact the **plot**. Each one should serve a narrative purpose. Maybe they provide a crucial piece of information. Maybe they betray the protagonist at the worst possible moment. Maybe they die halfway through the story, raising the stakes and forcing the protagonist to change course.

You can use ChatGPT to plan this quickly. Ask, "What key plot function can this supporting character serve in the story?" It will help you define why each character exists and how they move the story forward.

Another important trick is to make your supporting characters memorable, even if they only appear briefly. Give them quirks, unique voices, or distinct personalities. You don't need pages of backstory—just enough detail to make them feel like real people.

ChatGPT can help you with that too. Ask, "Give me three personality traits and one unusual habit for this character." Suddenly, your informant isn't just a plot device—they're a chain-smoking bartender with a photographic memory and a habit of quoting Shakespeare.

And let's not forget about red herrings. In a thriller, some of your supporting characters should deliberately mislead the protagonist—and the reader. Maybe they act suspicious but aren't actually guilty. Maybe they seem helpful but have their own selfish reasons. These false leads are part of the fun and tension of the genre.

You can ask ChatGPT, "Which supporting character could serve as a red herring in this story? How can I make them seem guilty without actually being guilty?" This will help you plant misdirection without confusing or frustrating the reader.

Finally, think about the emotional impact of your supporting characters. In a thriller, readers need to care about more than just the plot—they need to care about the people. If one of your supporting characters dies, betrays the protagonist, or disappears mysteriously, it should hit hard. The best way to make that happen is to make these characters matter to your protagonist.

Use ChatGPT to brainstorm quick scenes or moments that show the relationships between the protagonist and their allies or obstacles. Ask, "Give me a scene idea that shows the bond between the protagonist and this character," or "How can I create tension between these two characters early in the story?"

By the time you're done crafting your supporting characters, you should have a small but powerful cast of allies, informants, skeptics, obstacles, and red herrings who all serve the story and the protagonist's journey.

And because you're using ChatGPT, you can do this in a fraction of the time it would normally take. No more spending weeks inventing side characters who don't matter. You'll build a supporting cast that's lean, purposeful, and unforgettable—all in one writing session.

In the next chapter, we're going to step back and look at the bigger picture: understanding thriller genre subtypes and how they can shape the story you're about to write.

Understanding Thriller Genre Subtypes

By now, you've got your ending mapped out, your protagonist and antagonist crafted, and your supporting characters ready to bring the story to life. But before you dive headfirst into writing your thriller in one day, there's one more piece of the puzzle you need to think about—**what kind of thriller are you writing?** Because not all thrillers are built the same. There are several subtypes within the thriller genre, and knowing which one you're writing will help shape the tone, pacing, characters, and story beats.

Understanding these subtypes also helps you lean into the specific expectations that readers of thrillers are craving. It's not enough to just throw danger and tension onto the page—you want to deliver the specific kind of thrill your audience is looking for.

The good news is, you don't have to waste time trying to figure this out on your own. You can use ChatGPT to help you explore and lock in the best thriller subtype for your story idea. But first, let's break down the major types.

One of the most popular thriller subtypes is the **Psychological Thriller**. These stories aren't focused on explosions or car chases—they're built on tension, manipulation, and mind games. The danger here is often internal. The protagonist might be unraveling mentally, questioning reality, or trapped in a web of lies and secrets. Think of films like *Shutter Island* or *Gone Girl*. If your story is all about doubt, obsession, paranoia, and blurred lines between truth and illusion, you're probably writing a psychological thriller.

Then there's the **Action Thriller**, which is fast, physical, and intense. These stories often involve clear threats like terrorists, assassins, or criminal organizations, and they keep the protagonist constantly on the move. The pacing is relentless, the stakes are high, and there's usually a lot of danger in every scene. Think of movies like *The Bourne Identity* or *Taken*. If your protagonist is running, fighting, or being hunted, you're probably writing an action thriller.

Another subtype is the **Crime Thriller**, which usually blends the mystery of a whodunit with the pace and tension of a thriller. The plot typically revolves around a crime—often murder—and the protagonist is trying to solve it while also racing against time, facing threats, or being in danger themselves. *Se7en*, *Zodiac*, and *Prisoners* are good examples. If your story revolves around an investigation with rising stakes, this is your lane.

The **Political Thriller** is all about conspiracies, government secrets, espionage, and power struggles. These stories often involve big institutions, corrupt officials, and protagonists caught in a dangerous web of lies. *The Manchurian Candidate* or *The Parallax View* fall into this category. If your protagonist is up against the system itself, you're writing a political thriller.

You also have the **Legal Thriller**, where the courtroom is the battlefield. The tension isn't just in physical danger but in the manipulation of the law, secrets from the past, and high-stakes legal battles. *The Firm* or *A Time to Kill* are classic examples. If your story revolves around lawyers, courtrooms, and legal danger, that's your niche.

Another powerful subtype is the **Techno-Thriller**. These stories are fueled by cutting-edge technology, espionage, and global consequences. Think of *Enemy of the State* or *Blackhat*. The protagonist is often racing against a digital or technological threat that has real-world, devastating consequences.

Then there's the **Domestic Thriller**, which has become hugely popular in recent years. These stories are smaller in scale but emotionally intense. The danger comes from within relationships—spouses, neighbors, family, friends. Betrayal, lies, secrets, and psychological manipulation are at the core. *The Girl on the Train* and *Big Little Lies* fit here. If your thriller is about the darkness hiding behind closed doors, you're in domestic thriller territory.

There's also the **Survival Thriller**, where the protagonist isn't fighting a villain so much as fighting to survive against overwhelming odds. It might be nature, isolation, a killer on the loose, or even their own mind. *The Revenant*, *Buried*, or *127 Hours* are all survival thrillers. If your story is about one person versus the world, this is your category.

So why does it matter which subtype you're writing? Because each subtype comes with its own tone, pacing, types of characters, and storytelling style. If you don't know which one you're writing, your story will feel scattered. You'll waste time chasing plot ideas that don't fit and crafting scenes that don't deliver the specific kind of tension your readers want.

The easiest way to decide is to look at the story concept and ending you've already built. Ask yourself, "What kind of tension is at the heart of this story? What kind of threat drives the plot?" Then use ChatGPT to help you lock in the subtype. You can prompt, "Based on this story concept, which thriller subtype fits best and why?" It'll give you a clear answer.

Once you know your subtype, you can use it as a creative filter. When you're building your scenes, crafting dialogue, or adding twists, you'll make decisions that align with the expectations of that thriller type. If you're writing a psychological thriller, you'll focus on uncertainty, paranoia, and emotional manipulation. If you're writing an action thriller, you'll lean into fast pacing, dangerous confrontations, and physical peril.

You can also use ChatGPT to help you understand the tropes and expectations of each subtype quickly. Try prompting, "List the key elements and tropes of a [chosen subtype] thriller." That way, you'll have a checklist to guide your writing session and make sure you're hitting all the right beats.

Knowing your thriller subtype will also help you later when you market and publish your story. Readers and publishers want to know exactly what kind of experience they're in for. If you can clearly say, "This is a domestic thriller about secrets, betrayal, and revenge," or "This is a techno-thriller about a cyber-attack that could bring down a nation," you'll immediately attract the right audience.

But most importantly, it helps you write faster. When you have a clear framework—your ending, your protagonist and antagonist, your supporting characters, and your specific thriller subtype—you can blaze through your writing session without stopping to wonder what tone, style, or tension you should aim for. It's all locked in.

The Power of Conflict in a Thriller Story

If you strip a thriller story down to its bones, one word remains: conflict. It's the heartbeat of the genre. Conflict is what generates tension, accelerates pacing, reveals character, and keeps the reader leaning forward instead of setting your story down. In a thriller, conflict isn't optional—it's the engine. Without it, nothing moves. And if you're trying to write a thriller in one day, then understanding how to use conflict effectively is your shortcut to gripping storytelling.

Now, a lot of new writers confuse conflict with just "action" or "violence," but conflict is a much broader concept. At its core, conflict is about opposition. It's about one force pushing against another. And in a thriller, you want that push to be intense, urgent, and always escalating.

There are three main layers of conflict that should show up in your thriller: external conflict, internal conflict, and interpersonal conflict. These layers work together to create a complex, fast-moving story that resonates emotionally and keeps readers hooked from the first scene to the last.

Let's start with external conflict, which is what most people think of when they imagine a thriller. This is the danger. The physical threat. The race against time. The serial killer, the bomb, the government conspiracy, the stalker, the plane crash. This is the big, loud, visible part of the story, and it's what puts your protagonist in real jeopardy.

ChatGPT is fantastic for building this kind of conflict quickly. You can prompt it with, "Give me five external threats that could drive a thriller story," or, "What kind of danger could this protagonist be running from?" Within seconds, you'll have a list of possible conflicts you can fold into your story.

But external conflict alone isn't enough to make a thriller feel rich. That's where internal conflict comes in. Your protagonist should be dealing with some kind of emotional, psychological, or moral struggle at the same time they're dodging danger. Maybe they don't trust themselves. Maybe they've done something terrible in the past. Maybe they're torn between doing what's right and doing what's necessary.

This internal conflict adds depth. It makes the protagonist relatable. It also turns every decision into a source of tension—not just because of the external threat, but because they're battling themselves too.

You can ask ChatGPT, "What's a compelling internal conflict for a protagonist in this story?" or "How can this character's flaw make their situation even more dangerous?" Use the AI to layer these emotions in quickly. You'll end up with a character who feels real, even in extreme situations.

Then there's interpersonal conflict—the friction between characters. Allies argue. Friends betray. Enemies make surprising alliances. A great thriller thrives on complicated relationships. The protagonist might be working with someone they don't trust. They might have to protect someone who slows them down. Or they might discover that someone they love is actually working against them.

This interpersonal layer brings drama, doubt, and a lot of juicy dialogue. It's also a great place to surprise the reader. Someone who seems like an ally early on turns out to have an agenda. Someone who seems untrustworthy ends up saving the day.

ChatGPT can help you craft these dynamics fast. Try asking, "What tension could exist between this protagonist and their partner?" or "How can I create conflict between the protagonist and a key supporting character?" You'll quickly generate ideas for betrayal, miscommunication, jealousy, competition, or deep-seated grudges.

Here's the real trick: these three levels of conflict—external, internal, and interpersonal—should all overlap and escalate together. That's how you create a story that feels full, intense, and constantly in motion. As the external danger gets worse, the protagonist's internal struggle gets harder to ignore. As their world crumbles, their relationships strain and snap. The tension doesn't come in waves—it stacks.

And that stacking effect is what keeps your reader turning pages. They're not just asking, "Will the protagonist survive?" They're asking, "Can they hold themselves together?" "Can they trust anyone?" "Will they make the right choice, or fall apart?" That's thriller gold.

Let's talk for a second about escalation. Conflict in a thriller should never stay flat. Every time your protagonist gets closer to solving the mystery or escaping the threat, something should go wrong. A new problem arises. An ally is taken out. The villain makes a move. The internal pressure rises. The reader should feel like things are getting worse before they get better.

You can use ChatGPT to help structure this. Try prompts like, "How can I raise the stakes in Act Two of this thriller?" or "What plot twist could throw the protagonist off balance at the midpoint?" You'll get instant suggestions that make your story more intense and unpredictable.

Another way to keep conflict fresh is to create **moral conflict**—put your protagonist in situations where every option is bad. Do they save one person and let another die? Do they break the law to do the right thing? Do they trust the enemy to get what they need? These dilemmas are thrilling because they force the reader to ask, "What would I do?" It pulls them into the story emotionally.

You can ask ChatGPT to generate moral dilemmas that fit your specific plot. A simple prompt like, "What moral choice could this character face in the final act of a thriller?" can give you all kinds of high-stakes decisions that will elevate your story.

And don't forget about the ticking clock. Time pressure is one of the most effective forms of conflict in a thriller. A bomb is going off. The killer is striking again in 24 hours. The evidence disappears at midnight. When time runs out, everything falls apart. This constant countdown adds urgency to every scene and forces the protagonist to act, even when they're not ready.

You can brainstorm time-based pressure points with ChatGPT using prompts like, "Give me three ways to add a ticking clock to this thriller story."

In the end, the goal isn't to overload your story with conflict just for the sake of it. The goal is to make sure every scene has **tension**. Whether it's a conversation, a car chase, or a moment of silence, something should always be pushing against the protagonist. That's what makes it a thriller. Not the bullets or the blood—but the unrelenting pressure.

And when you're writing the whole thing in one day, this clarity makes everything easier. You don't waste time wondering what should happen next. You just look at the story and ask, "Where's the conflict? How can I turn up the heat?"

In the next chapter, we're going to dive into structure—how to map your thriller using the classic three-act model, and how to make sure that structure keeps your conflict building all the way to the final blow.

Mapping Your Story Structure in Three Acts

If conflict is the heartbeat of your thriller, then structure is the skeleton. Without a clear structure, your story will wobble, meander, and eventually collapse under its own weight. But when you have a solid framework—especially the classic three-act structure—you'll be able to keep your story tight, focused, and thrilling all the way through. And when you're writing your thriller in one day, having this structure locked in before you start is going to save you hours of second-guessing and rewrites.

So, let's talk about how to use the three-act structure specifically for a thriller. It's simple, timeless, and works like a charm when you're trying to build a tense, high-stakes story in record time.

Act One: The Set-Up

The first act is where you introduce your world, your protagonist, and the conflict that's about to explode. In a thriller, Act One is all about **disruption**. You start by showing the protagonist's normal life—or at least, their status quo—and then you shatter it with an inciting incident.

The inciting incident is what kicks the story into gear. It's the moment when the protagonist is pulled into danger, mystery, or conflict. Someone dies. Something is stolen. A body turns up. A secret is revealed. This is the hook that grabs the reader and says, "Buckle up. Things are about to get bad."

You can use ChatGPT to help you brainstorm a killer inciting incident. Try a prompt like, "What is a high-stakes inciting incident for a thriller about [your protagonist]?"

Once the inciting incident hits, Act One should keep escalating. The protagonist is forced to react, make choices, and start uncovering clues. But there's one key turning point you want to hit before Act One ends: the **First Major Plot Point**. This is the moment when your protagonist fully commits to the fight. There's no going back. They've crossed a line, made a choice, or been dragged so deep into danger that the only way out is through.

By the end of Act One, your reader should know exactly what the protagonist wants, what's at stake, and what's standing in their way. You're lighting the fuse on the bomb, and now you're going to watch it burn.

Act Two: The Confrontation

Act Two is the biggest section of your thriller, and it's where most writers get lost. But when you break it down, it's just the middle of the chess game—the back-and-forth between protagonist and antagonist, with the stakes rising at every turn.

This is where your protagonist starts **actively pursuing their goal**. They're investigating, running, fighting, piecing together the puzzle. But every time they get close to the truth, something goes wrong. A new obstacle appears. An ally betrays them. The villain stays one step ahead.

Act Two should feel like a rising staircase of tension. Each step gets harder. Each setback hurts more. Each discovery reveals a bigger problem.

One of the most important moments in Act Two is the **Midpoint Twist**. This is the moment that flips the entire story on its head. The protagonist learns something shocking. A key character is killed. The true villain is revealed. Or the protagonist's goal shifts completely.

You can ask ChatGPT, "What's a strong midpoint twist for a thriller story about [your concept]?" This will give you options to choose from or inspire your own.

After the midpoint, Act Two becomes even more intense. Your protagonist is running out of time, options, and allies. This is where their internal conflict hits hardest. They doubt themselves. They make mistakes. The antagonist tightens the noose.

Act Two ends with the **Second Major Plot Point**—a devastating blow that sets up the climax. Maybe the protagonist is betrayed. Maybe the villain wins a crucial victory. Maybe the protagonist loses someone they care about. This is the low point, the dark night of the soul.

Act Three: The Resolution

Act Three is the shortest and fastest-moving part of your thriller. This is where everything explodes. The tension you've been building finally pays off.

Your protagonist is at rock bottom—but now they make one final choice. They find the last piece of the puzzle. They rally. They confront the villain.

This is the climax—the showdown. Whether it's a rooftop fight, a courtroom reveal, or a tense conversation with a ticking clock, this is the scene your whole story has been building toward. It should be intense, emotional, and decisive.

Once the climax is over, you tie up loose ends in the resolution. Show the aftermath. Show how the protagonist has changed. Give your reader a moment to breathe after the rollercoaster ride.

When you're writing your thriller in one day, having this structure in front of you is essential. You don't have to figure out what happens next—you already know. You're just filling in the details, building the scenes, and keeping the pace tight.

You can also use ChatGPT to help you outline your thriller quickly. Try prompting, "Give me a three-act structure outline for a thriller story about [your concept]." In seconds, you'll have a full roadmap to follow.

Here's why this matters: writing a thriller isn't about guessing your way through the story. It's about tension, pacing, and escalation. The three-act structure gives you the framework to do that without wasting time.

It also keeps you from getting stuck. Every time you hit a wall, you can look at your structure and know exactly where you are. You'll see if you're still in Act One, climbing toward the first major plot point. Or if you're deep in Act Two, needing to raise the stakes. Or if you're in Act Three, racing toward the final showdown.

And because you're writing fast, you can use the structure as your safety net. You can make bold creative choices without worrying that the story will fall apart. You've got a framework holding everything together.

In the next chapter, we're going to break this structure down even further and outline the key plot points you'll need to hit in each act to keep your thriller tight, thrilling, and satisfying.

Outlining the Major Thriller Plot Points

Now that you've got the three-act structure in your toolkit, it's time to drill down and get specific. Structure is great, but what actually happens in each act is what makes a thriller tick. You need a clear, purposeful sequence of plot points that will drive your protagonist, escalate the tension, and keep the reader breathless until the very end.

The best part? When you outline these major plot points in advance, writing your thriller in one day becomes easy. You won't waste time wondering what should happen next. You'll already have the roadmap, and all you'll need to do is fill in the gaps.

So let's walk through the key plot points that every gripping thriller should hit—and how you can quickly outline them using ChatGPT.

Act One: The Set-Up and Inciting Incident

The first major plot point is your **Inciting Incident**. This is the moment that punches a hole in the protagonist's ordinary world and throws them into chaos. It might be a murder, a kidnapping, a shocking betrayal, or the discovery of a dark secret. This is the hook—the moment where the reader and protagonist both realize that something is very wrong.

Use ChatGPT to brainstorm your inciting incident fast. Try, "Give me five possible inciting incidents for a thriller about [your concept]." Choose the one that's most surprising and forces your protagonist to take action.

Next, you'll need to establish **The Key Players**—the antagonist, supporting characters, and the protagonist's goal. Readers should understand who's against your protagonist, who's helping them, and what's at stake. By the end of Act One, your protagonist should make a choice or take an action that commits them to the journey. That's your **First Major Plot Point**. It's the point of no return.

Act Two: Rising Tension and Major Reversals

Act Two is where the fun really begins. Your protagonist is now in the thick of the conflict, and things should get worse with every chapter.

The first key plot point in Act Two is the **First Major Obstacle**. This is where your protagonist faces an unexpected complication that throws their plan off course. Maybe a key witness disappears. Maybe their closest ally turns out to be working for the antagonist. You want to show that this journey will not be easy.

Use ChatGPT to brainstorm obstacles. Prompt it with, "What obstacle could derail my protagonist's investigation or plan?"

Next comes the **Midpoint Twist**—the turning point of the entire story. Something big happens here. The protagonist discovers a shocking truth, suffers a devastating loss, or realizes that everything they thought they knew was wrong. This moment changes the direction of the story and raises the stakes to a whole new level.

You can ask ChatGPT, "What would be a jaw-dropping midpoint twist for this thriller story?"

After the midpoint, the conflict accelerates. You'll want to include **Escalating Setbacks**—moments where the antagonist tightens their grip and the protagonist's situation becomes more desperate. Maybe the protagonist is framed for a crime. Maybe the villain kidnaps someone they love. Maybe a betrayal from a trusted ally sends them spiraling.

Another key plot point in Act Two is the **Darkest Moment**, also called the Second Major Plot Point. This is where everything falls apart. The protagonist hits rock bottom. Their plan has failed. The antagonist seems unstoppable. All hope is lost.

ChatGPT can help you craft this moment quickly. Try, "What would be a devastating low point for this protagonist?"

Act Three: Climax and Resolution

The third act is where everything comes to a head.

The first major plot point here is the **Final Discovery or Revelation**. This is when the protagonist figures out the last crucial piece of the puzzle—something that allows them to finally confront the antagonist. It might be a hidden truth, a realization about themselves, or a piece of evidence they overlooked.

Ask ChatGPT, "What final revelation could help the protagonist defeat the antagonist?"

Then comes the **Climax**—the ultimate showdown between protagonist and antagonist. This is the scene your entire story has been building toward. It should be tense, fast, and decisive. Whether it's a physical confrontation, a psychological battle, or a race against time, the climax should be unforgettable.

You can prompt ChatGPT with, "Describe a tense and thrilling climax scene for this story."

Finally, you'll need a **Resolution**. After the dust settles, what's the aftermath? How has the protagonist changed? What's the cost of their victory? You don't need to tie everything up neatly, but your story should feel complete.

Use ChatGPT to brainstorm your resolution. Ask, "How can I show the emotional impact of this story's ending on the protagonist?"

Putting It All Together

Here's a quick example of how your outline might look after mapping out the major plot points:

- **Act One:** Protagonist's ordinary world → Inciting incident → Introduce antagonist and allies → First major plot point (protagonist commits to the journey)
- **Act Two:** First major obstacle → Rising tension → Midpoint twist → Escalating setbacks → Darkest moment
- **Act Three:** Final discovery → Climax showdown → Resolution

Once you've got these points outlined, you're ready to write your thriller story in one day. You don't have to stop and figure out what happens next—you already know. And with ChatGPT by your side, you can brainstorm, tweak, and refine each plot point in minutes.

This is the magic of working smart. Instead of wandering through your story, you're building it with purpose and momentum. You'll move from blank page to finished thriller faster than you ever thought possible.

The Midpoint Twist and How to Make It Hit Hard

If there's one moment in your thriller story that can flip everything upside down and leave your reader gasping, it's the **midpoint twist**. This is the pivot point of your entire narrative. It's the jolt of electricity that reminds the reader they're not safe, that what they thought was happening isn't the full story, and that things are about to get much worse.

The midpoint twist isn't just another plot point—it's a tool to re-ignite your story's tension and force your protagonist (and reader) to question everything. And when you're writing your thriller in one day, knowing what this twist is from the start will make the entire middle of your story easier to write, because you'll know exactly what you're building toward.

So, what exactly is the midpoint twist? In simple terms, it's a revelation, event, or reversal that fundamentally changes the trajectory of your story. It can be a major plot reveal, a character betrayal, a devastating loss, or a game-changing discovery. It doesn't end the conflict—it deepens it. It's the moment when the protagonist realizes they've been wrong, misled, or underestimated the danger they're facing.

Think of it like this: Act One is the setup. Act Two begins with the protagonist reacting to the inciting incident and trying to solve the problem. But at the midpoint, the rules of the game change. The ground shifts beneath the protagonist's feet. And from that point on, they're not just reacting—they're fighting to survive.

Let's look at a few classic examples. In *The Silence of the Lambs*, the midpoint twist is when Clarice Starling realizes that the FBI's assumptions about the killer are wrong—that they've been chasing the wrong leads. In *Gone Girl*, the midpoint twist is the infamous reveal that Amy is alive and has staged her own disappearance. In *The Bourne Identity*, the midpoint comes when Jason Bourne learns how deep the conspiracy around him really goes.

In every case, the twist isn't random—it's something that grows naturally out of the story but forces the protagonist to reassess everything.

When you're writing your thriller in one day, you don't have time to stumble upon this twist by accident. You need to design it up front. And this is where ChatGPT becomes your secret weapon.

Start by looking at your story's concept and ending. What's the truth your protagonist doesn't know yet? What secret is hiding in plain sight? You can ask ChatGPT, "What possible midpoint twists could flip this thriller story on its head?" or "What hidden truth could my protagonist discover halfway through the story?"

You'll instantly get a list of possible twists. Pick one that feels like it will make your protagonist's life hell.

Here's a good rule of thumb when crafting your midpoint twist: it should either reveal something shocking about the **plot**, the **antagonist**, or the **protagonist** themselves.

A plot twist might expose a hidden agenda. Maybe the protagonist realizes they've been chasing the wrong person. Maybe the crime they're trying to solve is actually part of a much larger conspiracy.

A character twist might reveal that an ally is actually an enemy—or that the antagonist has a personal connection to the protagonist. This adds emotional weight and complicates every decision.

An internal twist is when the protagonist discovers something about themselves that changes how they see the conflict. Maybe they've been manipulated. Maybe they're more responsible for the chaos than they realized. Maybe their own flaw is what's putting everyone in danger.

You can use ChatGPT to brainstorm variations of these categories quickly. Try prompting, "Give me five possible midpoint twists based on the protagonist discovering something about themselves."

Another technique to make your midpoint twist hit hard is to make it **personal**. A plot twist is fine, but a personal betrayal, loss, or revelation hits readers in the gut. If you can tie the twist to your protagonist's emotional arc, it will resonate more deeply.

For example, if your protagonist's flaw is that they don't trust anyone, the midpoint twist could be discovering that the one person they let in has been lying to them all along. That kind of twist doesn't just escalate the plot—it tears at the protagonist's very soul.

Once you've chosen your twist, map out how it affects the rest of the story. A great midpoint twist creates a ripple effect. It doesn't just shock the reader—it changes the protagonist's goals, relationships, and strategies. It raises the stakes and accelerates the pacing.

Ask ChatGPT, "What impact will this twist have on the protagonist's decisions in Act Two?" or "How can I escalate the conflict after this twist?"

You should also think about how you'll **set up** the twist without giving it away. The best twists aren't pulled out of nowhere—they're hiding in plain sight. You drop subtle hints, plant red herrings, and lead the reader to think they know what's going on—until you pull the rug out from under them.

You can use ChatGPT to help you plant these clues. Prompt it with, "How can I foreshadow this midpoint twist without making it obvious?" It will give you ideas for character behavior, dialogue, or background details that will make the twist feel both surprising and inevitable.

Another way to make your twist hit hard is to time it well. The midpoint twist should fall around the halfway mark of your story—not too early, not too late. In a typical three-act structure, it's the pivot that turns Act Two from reaction to confrontation. When you're writing your thriller in one day, aim to hit the midpoint around the halfway mark of your draft.

And don't be afraid to go big. This is the moment to shock your reader. Kill off a major character. Reveal a betrayal. Flip the story upside down. The bigger the twist, the more thrilling the second half of your story will be.

Here's an example. Let's say your protagonist is hunting a serial killer. At the midpoint, they discover that the killer is someone they know—a family member, an old friend, or even their own partner. That twist doesn't just change the plot—it throws the protagonist into emotional turmoil and forces them to make impossible choices.

Or maybe your story is about a corporate conspiracy. The midpoint twist is that the protagonist's boss—the person who's been helping them—is actually the one pulling the strings. Suddenly, the protagonist is alone, outmatched, and questioning everything.

Once you've designed your twist, bake it into your outline. Make sure every scene leading up to it is building tension and planting clues. Then, when you hit that midpoint, drop the bomb and let the story explode in a new direction.

How to Weave Suspense through Every Scene

When readers pick up a thriller, they're not looking for calm, comfortable storytelling. They're looking for that delicious feeling of unease, of tension tightening like a rope around their chest, making them desperate to know what happens next. And the secret to creating that experience isn't just in the plot twists or the action-packed climax—it's in the suspense you weave through **every single scene**.

Suspense isn't something you sprinkle on top at the end like sugar on a cake. It's baked into the batter. It's the invisible thread that connects every moment in your thriller, pulling the reader deeper and deeper until they can't stop reading. So if you want to write your thriller in one day, you need to learn how to weave that tension consistently, and the good news is, it's easier than you think—especially when you've got ChatGPT to help you.

First, let's clear up what suspense actually is. Suspense is **the anticipation of something bad happening.** It's the space between a threat being introduced and the moment it either strikes or is narrowly avoided. It's what keeps the reader's heart rate up, even when nothing outwardly dangerous is happening in the scene.

One of the best ways to create suspense is to make sure the reader always knows **something the protagonist doesn't**. This is called dramatic irony, and it's a classic technique used by thriller writers and filmmakers alike. If the reader knows there's a bomb under the table but the protagonist doesn't, every innocent conversation becomes unbearably tense. You can use ChatGPT to brainstorm moments like this quickly. Try prompting, "How can I create dramatic irony in this scene?"

Another technique is to **withhold information**—but not in a frustrating way. You want to give the reader just enough to keep them guessing, but not so much that they can predict the ending. Every scene should leave them with a question: What's going to happen next? Who can be trusted? What's really going on?

You can use ChatGPT to help you structure this. Ask, "What questions can I plant in this scene to keep the reader guessing?" The AI will give you options for foreshadowing, red herrings, and character behavior that will fuel the suspense.

One of the most powerful ways to weave suspense is to use the **ticking clock** device. Time pressure is a classic thriller element because it naturally creates tension. If the protagonist only has an hour to stop the bomb, or two days to find the missing person, every scene becomes urgent. But the ticking clock doesn't always have to be literal. It can be emotional. Maybe the protagonist is running out of time to prove their innocence. Maybe the villain is getting closer to their goal with every passing moment.

Ask ChatGPT, "How can I add a ticking clock element to this story?" and you'll get instant ideas for time-based tension.

You should also build suspense by focusing on **small, immediate threats**, not just the big-picture danger. Every scene should have a source of tension, even if it's something subtle. Maybe it's a tense conversation. Maybe it's the protagonist sneaking through a dark hallway, knowing the villain could be around the corner. Maybe it's the protagonist making a risky decision and not knowing if it will backfire.

Use ChatGPT to help you brainstorm these scene-level threats. Prompt, "What small, immediate threat can I add to this scene to increase suspense?"

Another essential ingredient in suspense is **unanswered questions.** Your story should be full of mysteries, but you don't want to answer them too quickly. When you resolve one question, introduce another. Keep the reader on a leash, pulling them from one mystery to the next.

For example, if your protagonist finds out who killed the victim, reveal that the murder was just the tip of the iceberg. If they discover the villain's plan, reveal that there's a bigger conspiracy behind it. Always keep one step ahead.

You can use ChatGPT to help pace these reveals. Try, "How can I structure the reveals in this thriller to keep the suspense building?"

Suspense also comes from the **characters' emotions**. Don't just describe what's happening—show how the protagonist is reacting. Fear, doubt, anger, confusion—these emotions should bleed through every scene. The reader should feel what the protagonist feels.

You can use ChatGPT to help you layer in these emotional beats quickly. Ask, "How can I show the protagonist's fear and doubt in this scene?"

One mistake writers often make is thinking suspense has to mean constant action. It doesn't. Some of the most suspenseful scenes are quiet, slow, and tense. Think of a scene where two characters are having a polite conversation, but the reader knows one of them is lying. That's suspense. It's the tension beneath the surface that keeps the reader on edge.

When writing your thriller in one day, you can use ChatGPT to inject this kind of subtext into your dialogue. Prompt, "Write tense dialogue between these two characters where one is hiding something."

And don't forget the power of **setting** in building suspense. A dark alley, an abandoned building, a crowded train station—locations can add tension just by their atmosphere. Use sensory details to make the reader feel the danger closing in.

Ask ChatGPT, "Describe a suspenseful setting for this scene," and you'll get atmospheric descriptions you can drop straight into your story.

Another trick to sustain suspense is to use **cliffhangers** at the end of scenes or chapters. Don't resolve every conflict neatly. End on a moment of doubt, danger, or discovery. Force the reader to keep going.

You can prompt ChatGPT with, "Write a cliffhanger ending for this chapter," and you'll get quick, punchy lines to hook the reader.

The most important thing to remember is that suspense is about **unresolved tension**. Keep the reader's anxiety simmering. Make them worry. Make them question. Make them feel like something bad is always just around the corner.

When you master the art of weaving suspense through every scene, your thriller will feel unstoppable. Readers won't be able to put it down—not because of one big twist or explosive climax, but because you've made them lean in, page after page, wondering what's coming next.

Using Red Herrings, Misdirection, and Foreshadowing

There's a simple truth about writing thrillers that every professional knows but a lot of beginners overlook: the real game isn't just what happens—it's what the reader **thinks is happening**. In a great thriller, you're not just telling a story. You're playing with the reader's mind. You're leading them down dark alleys, pointing their attention one way while the real danger lurks in the shadows. And the tools you use to do that are **red herrings, misdirection, and foreshadowing**.

If you want your thriller to snap and crackle with tension—especially when you're writing it in one day—these techniques will make the difference between a predictable story and one that keeps readers guessing until the last page.

Let's start with **red herrings**. A red herring is a false clue. It's information, behavior, or an event that leads the protagonist—and the reader—to suspect the wrong person, anticipate the wrong outcome, or draw the wrong conclusion. In other words, it's deliberate misdirection.

Red herrings are like magic tricks. You show the audience one thing to distract them from what's really going on. If your thriller is a murder mystery, you might introduce a character who has a motive, behaves suspiciously, and seems to have everything to gain—but in the end, they're innocent. The red herring kept the reader's attention away from the real culprit.

When you're outlining your story, use ChatGPT to help you design these false leads quickly. Ask, "What red herring characters or clues can I add to mislead the protagonist?" You'll get ideas for suspicious behavior, misleading evidence, or even entire subplots designed to point your reader in the wrong direction.

But here's the key to a good red herring: it has to be **believable**. If the reader feels like you've tricked them unfairly, they'll be annoyed. The red herring has to make sense within the story. It has to feel like it could genuinely be the answer. That's why it's important to plant it carefully and make sure the false trail feels just as solid as the real one.

Next up is **misdirection**. Misdirection is similar to a red herring but broader. It's about controlling where the reader's attention goes. Sometimes it's done through dialogue. Sometimes it's through the way a scene is described. Sometimes it's through the order in which you reveal information.

A simple example: Your protagonist is searching a suspect's apartment, and you spend three paragraphs describing the messy living room, the suspicious pile of receipts, the locked drawer. Meanwhile, the real clue is sitting quietly on the kitchen table, mentioned once and easily overlooked.

Misdirection is also about making the reader trust the wrong characters or question the right ones. You can use ChatGPT to help you write dialogue or scenes that subtly shift suspicion. Ask, "How can I write this scene to mislead the reader without lying?"

One effective way to use misdirection is to **use your protagonist's point of view against them**. If your protagonist is certain that Character A is guilty, and the narrative follows their thoughts closely, the reader will naturally assume the same thing. But if your protagonist is missing something obvious—something you've carefully planted—the misdirection becomes even more powerful.

This is why thrillers are so fun to read and write. You're creating a puzzle and controlling how the reader pieces it together.

Finally, let's talk about **foreshadowing**. Where red herrings and misdirection are about leading the reader down the wrong path, foreshadowing is about subtly pointing to what's really coming. It's the art of planting seeds early in the story that pay off later. It's about making the reader feel like the ending was inevitable—without realizing why until it's too late.

Foreshadowing can be small and quiet. A throwaway line. A minor detail. A seemingly irrelevant moment. Later, when the twist is revealed, the reader looks back and realizes the clue was there all along.

When you're writing fast, you can use ChatGPT to help you plant these seeds quickly. Ask, "What subtle details can I add in Act One to foreshadow the final twist?" or "How can I hint at the protagonist's flaw in early scenes?"

The trick with foreshadowing is balance. Too obvious, and you give away the game. Too subtle, and it won't feel satisfying. The goal is to make the reader feel like they almost saw it coming—but didn't.

One smart strategy is to use foreshadowing to explain away things that don't seem important until they do. For example, if your protagonist is a detective who casually mentions an old case they never solved, that case could turn out to be connected to the villain's plan. Or if a character has an odd habit or fear early in the story, it could become crucial in the climax.

Another technique is to use **visual or sensory details** as foreshadowing. A broken lock, a photograph, a song playing on the radio—small things that seem incidental but later reveal deeper meaning.

Here's how you can put these three tools together:

Let's say your protagonist is hunting a serial killer. You introduce a neighbor who's shy, awkward, and has a dark past. You drop hints that they're hiding something. That's your red herring.

At the same time, you focus your story's attention on a string of physical clues that seem to point to this neighbor—but those clues were actually planted by someone else. That's misdirection.

And way back in Chapter Two, you mention in passing that the protagonist once worked undercover and had a partner who vanished without a trace. That detail doesn't seem important—until the midpoint twist reveals that the missing partner is the real killer. That's foreshadowing.

See how it works? You're playing three-dimensional chess with the reader. Red herrings distract them. Misdirection controls their attention. Foreshadowing lays the breadcrumbs that lead to the truth.

When you're writing your thriller in one day, you can use ChatGPT to brainstorm these techniques quickly and effectively. Instead of spending hours agonizing over how to mislead the reader, you can ask for ideas, scenes, dialogue, and details that will keep your story layered and unpredictable.

In the next chapter, we're going to turn to something just as important—**pacing**—and how to keep your thriller moving fast without burning out the reader or losing the tension.

Pacing: Keeping the Reader Hooked from Start to Finish

If there's one thing that separates an average thriller from a white-knuckle, can't-put-it-down, page-turning thriller, it's **pacing**. Pacing is what controls how the story unfolds. It's the rhythm of your scenes, the balance between action and quiet moments, the way you speed up when danger's close and slow down when emotions run high. Get the pacing right, and your readers won't even realize they're racing through your story. Get it wrong, and even the best plot in the world will feel like a slog.

The good news is that pacing isn't magic—it's a skill. And when you're writing your thriller in one day, understanding how to control pacing will help you keep momentum and finish strong without sacrificing quality.

So, how do you pace a thriller?

First, you need to understand that thrillers thrive on **urgency**. From the opening scene, the clock is ticking. Whether it's literal (a bomb, a deadline, a killer on the loose) or emotional (a secret that can't stay buried, a betrayal waiting to happen), the reader should feel a low-grade anxiety humming under every scene. They should feel like the story is always moving forward—like they can't stop because something terrible will happen if they do.

You can use ChatGPT to help you build that urgency right from the start. Ask, "What time pressure or looming threat can I add to this thriller story to keep the pacing tight?"

One of the best ways to maintain strong pacing is to structure your story around **rising tension**. Each scene should escalate the stakes, reveal new information, or create new obstacles. You never want your reader to feel like they're coasting. If the protagonist solves one problem, two more should pop up. If they catch their breath, the next threat should already be closing in.

You can use ChatGPT to help you plan this escalation. Try prompting, "How can I raise the stakes in each act of this thriller story?"

Another pacing trick is to **vary the rhythm**. Fast doesn't mean frantic. If every scene is a car chase or a shootout, readers will get exhausted. You need **breathing room**—moments of quiet tension, emotional reflection, or strategic planning. These slower moments give the reader a chance to process what's happening, catch their breath, and prepare for the next big hit.

Think of pacing like a rollercoaster. You have big drops, sharp turns, and a few slow climbs to build suspense. The balance is what keeps the ride thrilling.

ChatGPT can help you structure this flow. Prompt it with, "Help me balance high-tension scenes and slower moments in this thriller outline."

Another thing to pay attention to is **scene length**. Short, punchy scenes naturally speed up the pacing. Long, detailed scenes slow it down. In a thriller, you want to lean toward shorter scenes that end on cliffhangers, questions, or tension. This creates that addictive, "just one more chapter" effect.

You can also use **sentence structure** to control pacing. Short sentences. Sharp dialogue. Quick descriptions. These speed things up during action scenes. Longer, more descriptive sentences slow the reader down when you want to create mood or emotional depth.

When you're writing fast—trying to finish your thriller in one day—you can use ChatGPT to help you with this. Ask, "Rewrite this scene to make the pacing faster and more intense," or "Add tension to this dialogue without slowing down the pacing."

One of the biggest pacing mistakes thriller writers make is the dreaded **sagging middle**. You start strong. You have an exciting climax. But Act Two feels like wading through mud. That's because the middle is where most thrillers lose momentum.

The key to avoiding this is to pack the middle with **twists, reversals, and mini-climaxes**. Each time the protagonist thinks they're making progress, something unexpected should knock them off balance. Each time they find a clue, it should raise more questions. You can use ChatGPT to brainstorm these surprises. Prompt, "What plot twists can I add to keep the middle of this thriller tense and fast-paced?"

Another way to keep pacing tight is to **limit exposition**. Thriller readers don't want long backstories, info dumps, or pages of explanation. They want action, tension, and forward motion. Reveal information as the protagonist discovers it. Keep the reader learning alongside the characters, not ahead of them.

You can use ChatGPT to help you cut the fat. Ask, "How can I rewrite this exposition to reveal information through action or dialogue?"

And don't forget about **chapter endings**. In a thriller, every chapter should end with a question, a discovery, a threat, or a cliffhanger. Something that makes the reader turn the page. You can use ChatGPT to help craft these hooks. Prompt, "Write a cliffhanger ending for this chapter."

As you're writing your thriller in one day, pacing is your best friend. If you feel like the story is slowing down, look at the scene and ask: Is the protagonist actively pursuing their goal? Is there a new obstacle or threat? Is the reader learning something important? If the answer is no, the scene might need to go—or at least be rewritten to crank up the tension.

Pacing isn't just about speed. It's about **momentum**. It's about making sure every scene pulls the reader forward, whether it's a quiet conversation loaded with subtext or a high-speed chase through a dark city.

And the best part? You don't have to figure it out alone. You can use ChatGPT to help you structure, rewrite, and fine-tune your pacing scene by scene. It's like having a pacing consultant sitting next to you, ready to help whenever the story starts to drag.

Choosing the Right Setting for Maximum Tension

One of the most overlooked but absolutely essential ingredients in writing a gripping thriller is the **setting**. Most beginner writers think a thriller is all about plot twists, action, and dangerous characters—and yes, those things matter. But the setting is the invisible hand that amplifies the tension, builds atmosphere, and makes the reader feel trapped, uneasy, or breathless without even realizing why.

When you're writing your thriller story in one day, you might be tempted to treat setting as an afterthought. But if you choose the right locations and build them with purpose, they can do half the heavy lifting of creating suspense and tension for you.

So, how do you pick the right setting for your thriller? It all comes down to **limitation, isolation, and atmosphere**.

A great thriller setting isn't just a backdrop. It's a character. It actively shapes the tension, impacts the protagonist's choices, and creates obstacles. The best settings make the reader feel trapped, vulnerable, or like something bad is lurking around every corner.

Think about some of the most iconic thrillers you've seen or read. *The Silence of the Lambs* makes brilliant use of enclosed, claustrophobic spaces like the prison where Lecter is held. *Panic Room* is literally set inside a fortified room during a home invasion. *Shutter Island* isolates its characters on a storm-ravaged, eerie island psychiatric facility. The setting in each case isn't random—it's designed to make the characters' situation more dangerous and the reader's pulse race.

You can use ChatGPT to help you choose strong settings fast. Try prompting, "Suggest five thriller settings that would isolate the protagonist and increase tension."

When you're choosing your setting, ask yourself: **How can this location make things harder for my protagonist?** A dark alley, a remote cabin, a foreign city where they don't speak the language, an underground bunker—all of these naturally increase tension because they limit the protagonist's options, resources, or ability to escape.

Isolation is one of the best ways to crank up the pressure. When your protagonist is cut off from help, surrounded by enemies, or stuck in a place where nobody will believe them, the tension skyrockets. You can use physical isolation—like a blizzard-stranded mountain lodge—or social isolation—like being in a room full of people who may or may not want you dead.

But isolation isn't enough. The setting also needs to create a **mood**. You want locations that feel unsettling, claustrophobic, or unpredictable. Dark, stormy nights. Empty streets at midnight. Flickering neon lights in an underground club. Even ordinary settings can become creepy or tense if you describe them right.

Ask ChatGPT to help you bring your settings to life quickly. Prompt, "Describe a tense and atmospheric setting for a thriller scene in a city at night."

And here's a trick: don't overdescribe. Thriller pacing demands that your descriptions are lean, sharp, and sensory. You're not writing a travel brochure—you're painting tension with a few well-chosen details. Focus on sounds, shadows, smells, and the feeling of the place pressing in on your protagonist.

Another thing to think about is how you can use your setting to **trap** the protagonist. Maybe the antagonist controls the environment. Maybe the location itself becomes a threat—a burning building, a flooding tunnel, a collapsing skyscraper. When you make the setting dangerous, it forces your protagonist to act fast and keeps your reader on edge.

You can use ChatGPT to brainstorm ways to turn a location into a threat. Ask, "How can I make this setting dangerous and tense for the protagonist?"

One more important factor in choosing your setting is **contrast**. Sometimes the most chilling scenes happen in places that should feel safe. A quiet suburban street. A child's bedroom. A hospital corridor. When you put danger in a familiar or comfortable place, the tension is even higher because it violates the reader's sense of safety.

You can use this technique deliberately to unsettle the reader. Ask ChatGPT, "What familiar setting could I turn into a threatening location in this thriller story?"

Also, think about how the setting can serve the **themes** of your story. If your thriller is about paranoia and secrets, you might choose cold, sterile locations like corporate offices or government buildings. If your story is about personal betrayal, you might set key scenes in intimate, domestic spaces—homes, bedrooms, kitchens. The setting can subtly reinforce the emotional stakes.

When you're writing fast, ChatGPT can help you map this out. Prompt, "What settings would best match the themes of betrayal and paranoia in a thriller?"

Finally, use your setting to control the **pace** of your story. Small, contained settings naturally speed things up because there's nowhere to hide. Big, sprawling locations can slow things down and create a sense of dread or vast, inescapable danger.

You can even vary the setting within the story to control tension. Tight, confined spaces for action scenes. Open, eerie spaces for slower, tense moments.

Here's how you can put all of this together:

Let's say your story is about a detective trying to catch a serial killer. You could set key scenes in a dimly lit morgue, an abandoned subway tunnel, and the detective's own apartment—which is broken into by the killer midway through the story. Each setting serves the story. The morgue is cold and clinical, reinforcing the horror of the crimes. The subway tunnel is dark and claustrophobic, perfect for a chase scene. The detective's apartment feels safe—until it isn't.

In every case, the setting isn't just a location. It's a source of tension.

And when you're writing a thriller in one day, making these choices early will save you time. You can use ChatGPT to help you plan out the key locations, describe them vividly, and even brainstorm how to use the environment to trap, threaten, or mislead your protagonist.

In the next chapter, we'll talk about how to structure each scene so that every location, every character choice, and every moment drives the story forward without slowing the pace or wasting words.

Scene Structure – Making Every Scene Count

Thriller readers don't forgive wasted time. They don't want filler, they don't want fluff, and they definitely don't want scenes that lead nowhere. Every single scene in your thriller must do one thing—**count**. It has to push the story forward, reveal something important, raise the stakes, deepen a character, or tighten the tension. If it doesn't, cut it. And when you're writing your thriller in one day, making sure every scene earns its place is how you keep the pace fast and the reader hooked.

So, how do you structure a scene that actually matters?

First, understand that a scene is not just a chunk of writing. A scene is a **unit of conflict**. It's a building block of your thriller, and like every block, it has to be solid, sharp, and carefully placed.

Every scene should answer one or more of these questions:

- What new problem is introduced?
- What decision does the protagonist face?
- What obstacle is thrown in their way?
- What information is revealed?
- How does the tension escalate?

If your scene isn't answering at least one of those questions, you need to rethink it.

The basic structure of a great thriller scene has three simple parts: **Goal, Conflict, and Outcome**.

The protagonist enters the scene with a goal—something they want to achieve. That goal is immediately blocked by conflict—an obstacle, an antagonist, a new piece of information, or even their own fear or flaw. The scene ends with an outcome that's either a win, a loss, or something unexpected that forces them to change direction.

For example, let's say your protagonist is searching for a missing person. In one scene, their goal is to question a key witness. The conflict is that the witness refuses to talk—or worse, lies. The outcome is that the protagonist leaves frustrated but notices something in the witness's behavior that points them to the next clue. That's a scene that counts. It moves the story forward and keeps the tension high.

When you're writing quickly, you can use ChatGPT to help you structure scenes efficiently. Try prompting, "What is the protagonist's goal, conflict, and outcome in this scene?" The AI can help you clarify the purpose of each scene before you start writing, saving you time and energy.

Another crucial part of scene structure is **scene hooks** and **scene endings**. The first line of your scene should hook the reader. Drop them right in the middle of tension, mystery, or action. No long descriptions. No unnecessary build-up. Start with a bang, a question, or a conflict.

And just as importantly, don't let the scene drift off into nothing. End every scene with tension—an unanswered question, a new threat, a decision left hanging. That's what keeps readers turning the pages.

Use ChatGPT to help with this. Prompt, "Write an opening hook and cliffhanger ending for this scene."

You should also make sure that each scene is **anchored in a clear setting** and written from a specific character's point of view. Readers need to know where they are, who's there, and what's at stake. If a scene is vague, confusing, or meandering, it kills the pacing.

This doesn't mean every scene has to be an action sequence. Quiet scenes can be incredibly tense, especially if there's an undercurrent of danger, secrets, or conflict. A conversation can be as thrilling as a chase scene if the stakes are high enough.

Here's a practical example. Imagine a scene where your protagonist meets the antagonist for the first time, but doesn't know they're the villain yet. The setting is a busy café. The goal is to get information. The conflict is that the antagonist is evasive and charming. The outcome is that the protagonist leaves with a false sense of trust—but the reader knows better. The scene is tense, layered, and meaningful.

You can ask ChatGPT to help you structure scenes like this quickly. Prompt, "Outline a tense scene where the protagonist unknowingly meets the antagonist."

Another important technique in scene structure is to **keep the protagonist active**. They should be making choices, taking risks, reacting to danger. Don't let them drift through scenes like a spectator. They should drive the story, even when they're losing.

Each scene should also **build toward the next**. The outcome of one scene should naturally lead to the next goal, conflict, and outcome. This creates momentum and makes your story feel seamless.

When you're writing your thriller in one day, you can use ChatGPT to help map out this chain. Try prompting, "How can the outcome of this scene lead to the next conflict?"

It's also helpful to remember that not all scenes have to be the same length or intensity. Vary your scenes. Short, punchy scenes can speed things up. Longer, tense conversations can slow things down and add depth. Action scenes, investigative scenes, emotional scenes—all of them have a place, as long as they serve the story.

One thing you should avoid is scenes that repeat information or conflicts without adding anything new. If your protagonist learns something, they shouldn't have another scene where they learn the same thing again. Every scene should reveal something fresh, raise the stakes, or change the situation.

And finally, always keep your reader in mind. When they finish a scene, they should feel compelled to read the next one. That's the sign of a well-structured thriller scene.

Here's a simple workflow you can use when writing fast:

1. Use ChatGPT to outline the goal, conflict, and outcome of the scene.
2. Write the opening hook and closing cliffhanger.
3. Fill in the tension, dialogue, and action.
4. Make sure the scene either reveals new information, raises stakes, or forces the protagonist to act.
5. Move immediately to the next scene and repeat.

By following this structure, you can write sharp, tight scenes that keep the reader hooked—and finish your thriller draft in a single day without sacrificing quality.

How to Use Atmosphere and Environment to Build Dread

One of the most powerful tools in your thriller-writing arsenal isn't just what's happening—it's **how it feels while it's happening**. You can have all the action, plot twists, and dangerous characters you want, but if the reader doesn't feel a growing sense of unease crawling under their skin, your story won't leave a mark. That's where **atmosphere** and **environment** come in. These elements don't just set the scene—they shape the mood, stir anxiety, and build an inescapable sense of dread that keeps readers hooked.

Thrillers thrive on dread. Dread isn't the same as shock or surprise. It's the slow, gnawing feeling that something bad is coming and there's nothing anyone can do to stop it. It's that sinking sensation in the stomach, the tightening of the chest, the awareness that something's off—but not knowing exactly what. And the atmosphere you create with your settings, descriptions, and sensory details is what fuels that feeling.

When you're writing your thriller in one day, it's tempting to race through scenes, focusing only on action and dialogue. But if you slow down just enough to carefully craft atmosphere, you'll amplify the tension without adding unnecessary bulk to your story.

So, how do you use atmosphere and environment to build dread?

First, start by choosing the right **sensory details**. Readers don't just want to see the setting—they want to feel it. They want to smell the rain-soaked concrete, hear the distant sirens, feel the damp chill creeping under their skin. The more sensory layers you add, the more immersive and unsettling the scene becomes.

You don't need paragraphs of description. A few carefully chosen details can do the job. Instead of writing, "It was a dark night," show the reader the flickering streetlights, the greasy pavement slick with rain, the faint hum of something electric and broken in the air.

You can use ChatGPT to help you generate atmospheric descriptions quickly. Prompt, "Describe a tense, oppressive atmosphere in a dark alley at night," and you'll get instant mood-setting language you can drop into your scene.

Another technique is to use **environmental obstacles** to crank up the dread. Make the setting actively work against your protagonist. Maybe it's a snowstorm that blinds them, a power outage that plunges them into darkness, a labyrinthine building that disorients them. When the environment itself becomes a threat, it creates a constant sense of danger.

You can ask ChatGPT, "What environmental obstacles could heighten the tension in this thriller scene?" and use those suggestions to raise the stakes.

Also, think about how the **emotional state of your protagonist** is reflected in the environment. This is an old but effective technique called **pathetic fallacy**—using the setting to mirror what's happening internally. If your protagonist is unraveling, the world around them might feel chaotic, stormy, crumbling. If they're feeling trapped, the setting might be claustrophobic—a small, windowless room, a narrow alley, a crowded subway car.

You can use ChatGPT to brainstorm how to use setting to reflect emotion. Try, "How can I use the environment to reflect the protagonist's fear in this scene?"

The other essential part of atmosphere is what's **missing**. Silence, emptiness, absence of people or sound—these things can be just as powerful as loud, chaotic settings. An abandoned house, a quiet hallway, a dark, empty street. Stillness is unsettling in a thriller because it feels like something is about to happen. Readers lean forward in those moments, anticipating the danger lurking in the quiet.

You can also use **contrasting environments** to build dread. Place your characters in a setting that should feel safe—a cozy living room, a school, a family dinner—but layer in tension. Maybe the conversation is stiff, maybe a character's behavior feels off, maybe there's something just out of place. That contrast between safety and unease creates a slow-burn dread that can be more effective than outright horror.

Ask ChatGPT, "What ordinary setting could I make feel tense and dangerous in this thriller story?"

Another way to weaponize environment is to use **limited visibility**. Darkness, fog, thick crowds, closed doors—anything that restricts what the protagonist (and reader) can see ramps up the tension. When you can't see what's coming, your imagination fills in the worst possibilities.

Pair this with sound—creaks, footsteps, whispers, distant crashes—and you'll create an atmosphere thick with dread.

When writing fast, it's easy to overlook these atmospheric details, but you don't need to write pages of description. One or two well-placed lines per scene can change the entire mood. And ChatGPT can help you add them quickly. Ask, "Give me two lines of atmospheric description to increase tension in this scene."

Symbolism is another subtle tool you can use. Objects or environmental details that seem harmless at first but take on darker meaning as the story progresses. A ticking clock. A door that's always locked. A broken mirror. These details plant seeds of unease without spelling everything out.

You can even use the atmosphere to mislead the reader. Maybe you describe a peaceful, calm setting—then shatter it with sudden violence. Or you build an oppressive, eerie mood only to reveal nothing happens, keeping the reader on edge for the next scene.

Dread is about **anticipation**. The reader should constantly feel like something bad is coming, even if they don't know what or when. That's the thrill.

Here's a practical trick: When you finish writing a scene, take two minutes to reread it and ask yourself, "What's the mood here? How can I make it feel tenser?" Then use ChatGPT to help you add two or three sensory details, environmental obstacles, or atmospheric hints. It won't slow you down, and it will make your thriller feel rich, immersive, and genuinely unsettling.

Themes that Drive a Great Thriller

A lot of new writers think that thrillers are just about plot twists, action, and tension. And while those things are important—after all, you want readers flipping pages at midnight—what really makes a thriller memorable is the **theme** underneath the action. The theme is the heartbeat of your story. It's the deeper idea you're exploring, the question you're asking, the truth you're poking at while you lead the reader through a maze of danger and suspense.

Think of the theme as the **why** behind all the chaos. It's what makes your thriller stick in the reader's mind after they've finished the last page. It's what gives the story weight and meaning beyond the surface tension.

When you're writing your thriller story in one day, you might be tempted to skip over theme. But here's the secret: if you nail your theme early, it will actually make the entire writing process easier. Your theme will guide your characters' choices, your plot twists, and your ending. It gives you a compass so you're not just writing a bunch of disconnected action scenes—you're telling a story that resonates.

So, what kind of themes work well in thrillers?

One of the most common is the theme of **truth and deception**. Thrillers often revolve around lies, hidden motives, and secrets. Your protagonist is usually chasing the truth, and the antagonist is doing everything they can to keep it buried. But you can push this theme deeper. Ask yourself: What is the cost of truth? Does knowing the truth make life better—or worse? Is it possible that the protagonist is lying to themselves?

You can use ChatGPT to explore how this theme could shape your story. Ask, "How can I use the theme of truth and deception in this thriller plot?"

Another classic thriller theme is **justice versus revenge**. Is your protagonist seeking justice—or are they really after payback? And what's the difference? This theme adds emotional depth because it forces the protagonist (and the reader) to question their own morality. Are they doing the right thing, or just trying to even the score?

Think of stories like *The Girl with the Dragon Tattoo* or *Prisoners*, where characters blur the line between justice and revenge. If you choose this theme, you can build scenes where the protagonist has to make impossible choices between doing what's right and doing what feels good.

Another powerful thriller theme is **paranoia and trust**. In many thrillers, the protagonist can't trust anyone—not their allies, not their friends, not even themselves. This theme creates constant tension because the reader is always wondering who's lying, who's hiding something, and who will betray the protagonist next.

You can ask ChatGPT, "How can I weave a theme of paranoia and trust throughout this thriller story?" and get ideas for character relationships, plot twists, and internal conflict.

Power and corruption is another common theme. Thrillers often shine a light on how people in positions of authority abuse their power—and what happens when someone tries to expose them. This theme can apply to political thrillers, corporate thrillers, or even personal stories where one character holds power over another.

You can take this theme further by asking: How far will someone go to gain power? And what happens when they lose control?

Then there's the theme of **identity and self-discovery**. Many thrillers involve protagonists who are running from their past, hiding a secret, or questioning who they really are. Think of stories like *The Bourne Identity*, where the protagonist literally doesn't know who they are—and has to uncover their identity while fighting to survive.

This theme adds internal conflict and emotional stakes. You can use it to create moments where the protagonist's own fears and flaws become obstacles.

Survival and resilience is another key thriller theme. Whether your protagonist is physically fighting for their life or emotionally fighting to stay sane, the theme of survival adds weight to every scene. You can explore what people are willing to do to survive—and what it costs them in the end.

You can also choose a theme that's specific to your story's setting or premise. For example, if your thriller is about corporate espionage, the theme might be **greed and ambition**. If it's about a political conspiracy, the theme might be **freedom versus control**.

Here's the thing: You don't have to hammer the theme over the reader's head. You're writing a thriller, not a lecture. The theme should be woven subtly through the plot, the characters' choices, and the story's resolution. It should make the reader think, without slowing down the pace.

And when you're writing in one day, you can use ChatGPT to help you stay focused on your theme. At the start of your writing session, prompt: "What key scenes can I include to reinforce the theme of [insert theme]?" You'll get a list of ideas you can thread through your outline.

You can also use theme to shape your characters' arcs. Ask, "How can the protagonist's character arc reflect the theme of survival and resilience?" or "How can the antagonist embody the theme of power and corruption?"

Another smart move is to tie your theme to your **midpoint twist** and your **climax**. The twist should challenge the protagonist's belief about the theme, and the climax should force them to confront it head-on.

For example, if your theme is truth and deception, the midpoint twist might reveal that the protagonist has been lying to themselves all along. The climax might force them to decide whether they're willing to reveal an ugly truth—or keep living the lie.

By anchoring your plot points to your theme, you'll make your thriller feel cohesive and emotionally satisfying—even when you're writing it at top speed.

One final tip: choose a theme that **you** care about. When you're passionate about the underlying question your story is asking, it will bleed into every scene you write. Readers can feel that, even if they can't articulate why your thriller hits harder than others.

How to Write from a Thrilling Point of View

When you sit down to write a thriller, one of the most important decisions you'll make isn't about plot twists or who your villain is—it's about **point of view (POV)**. The POV you choose is the lens your reader experiences your story through, and in a thriller, that lens is everything. It controls how much information the reader gets, how tense the story feels, and how deep inside the protagonist's head the reader gets to crawl.

Most writers don't give enough thought to this. They jump into writing without realizing how much POV influences tension, pacing, and even the effectiveness of your plot twists. But if you get this right—especially when you're trying to write your thriller in one day—you'll find that everything else flows much easier. Because the right POV doesn't just tell the story. It **builds the suspense.**

So, let's break down the main POV choices you can use in your thriller—and how each one affects the tension.

The most common POV in modern thrillers is **third-person limited**. This means the narrator follows one character (usually the protagonist) closely, showing what they see, hear, think, and feel—but not what anyone else is thinking. Readers only know what the protagonist knows, which is perfect for building suspense.

Third-person limited is like watching the story over the protagonist's shoulder. It creates natural tension because readers only get pieces of the puzzle as the protagonist does. They discover clues, experience danger, and learn secrets at the same time. This POV is excellent for thrillers because it keeps the reader guessing without feeling cheated.

You can use ChatGPT to help you sharpen this voice. Try prompting, "Write this scene in third-person limited POV, focusing on the protagonist's fear and confusion."

If you want an even tighter connection between reader and character, you can choose **first-person POV**. This puts the reader directly inside the protagonist's head. Every thought, fear, and observation is filtered through their voice. First-person POV creates intimacy and urgency, which is why it's popular in psychological thrillers like *Gone Girl.*

The downside is that you're locked into one character's experience. You can't easily show what the antagonist is doing or give the reader information the protagonist doesn't have. But that can actually work in your favor because it limits what the reader knows and makes the story more claustrophobic.

If you go this route, use ChatGPT to capture the protagonist's voice fast. Prompt, "Write a tense first-person narration of this scene."

There's also **third-person omniscient**, where the narrator knows everything about everyone—their thoughts, feelings, and secrets. This POV can work in some thrillers, especially if you want to play with dramatic irony (where the reader knows something the protagonist doesn't). But it can also drain tension if not handled carefully, because readers know too much.

Most thrillers avoid full omniscient narration because it softens the mystery. However, you can strategically use it for certain scenes to show the villain's perspective or reveal information that tightens the suspense.

Speaking of villain perspective, many modern thrillers use a **dual POV** structure—switching between the protagonist and antagonist, or protagonist and a supporting character. This can be incredibly effective because it creates a cat-and-mouse dynamic. The reader gets glimpses of what the villain is planning, raising the stakes as the protagonist unknowingly walks into danger.

You can use ChatGPT to help outline this structure. Prompt, "How can I alternate POV between the protagonist and antagonist to build suspense?"

If you choose a dual POV, you have to be careful about how much you reveal. Give the reader enough to make them nervous, but not so much that you spoil the mystery. You want them yelling at the page, "No! Don't go in there!" because they know something the protagonist doesn't.

No matter which POV you choose, the key is to use it to **control information**. In a thriller, tension comes from what the reader doesn't know—or what they know that the characters don't. Your POV choice is your best tool for managing that flow of information.

Another important aspect of POV is **voice**. In first-person or close third-person, the character's voice should shape how the story is told. A jaded detective will narrate very differently from a terrified teenager. Their fears, flaws, and perspective color everything they see and how they react. That's what draws the reader in.

You can use ChatGPT to refine voice quickly. Ask, "Write this scene in the voice of a paranoid, exhausted detective in first-person."

When you're writing fast, it helps to decide early how close you want the reader to be to the protagonist's thoughts. Do you want them to feel every heartbeat, doubt, and breath? Or do you want them to watch from just behind the protagonist's shoulder? That choice will shape how you write every scene.

It's also worth thinking about **unreliable narrators**. First-person thrillers often use this technique, where the protagonist isn't telling the full truth—either because they're lying, confused, or delusional. This adds another layer of tension because the reader is constantly questioning what's real.

If you go this route, ChatGPT can help you craft subtle clues. Prompt, "How can I show that this narrator is unreliable without revealing it too soon?"

Finally, remember that POV affects **pacing**. A tight, limited POV keeps the tension close and personal. A broader POV can help you speed up exposition or show the bigger picture. Use your POV choice strategically to control how fast or slow the story feels.

When you're writing your thriller in one day, lock in your POV choice early. Write a quick sample scene from your protagonist's perspective and see if it feels right. If it doesn't, try another POV. Once you've found the voice and lens that makes the story sing, everything else will flow faster.

Playing with Reader Perception and Perspective

One of the coolest tricks you can pull off in a thriller—and one of the reasons thrillers are so addictive—is how you can **manipulate the reader's perception**. You're not just telling a story; you're playing a game with the audience's mind. You're giving them pieces of information, holding others back, nudging them toward the wrong conclusions, and flipping their expectations at the perfect moment. That's what makes thrillers feel like a rollercoaster: the sense that nothing is what it seems.

When you write a thriller in one day, this becomes one of your best tools because it lets you inject tension, mystery, and surprise without overcomplicating your plot. Instead of constantly inventing new twists, you can play with **how the reader perceives the story** and whose perspective they're locked into.

So, how do you control reader perception?

It starts with understanding that readers will believe what you show them. If you describe a character acting suspiciously, readers will assume they're guilty. If you withhold information, they'll fill in the blanks. If you plant a detail early, they'll remember it and expect it to matter later. You can use these natural reading habits to your advantage.

One simple technique is **selective focus**. You decide what the reader notices. You might spend three paragraphs describing a character's nervous behavior, leading the reader to think they're hiding something—when the real villain is in the background, barely mentioned. You might describe a scene from a certain angle, leaving out a crucial detail until later.

This is especially effective if you're writing in **first-person POV** or **third-person limited POV**. You can literally control what the protagonist notices and, by extension, what the reader perceives. If the protagonist is distracted, misinformed, or emotionally compromised, the reader is too.

You can use ChatGPT to help you sharpen this. Try prompting, "Rewrite this scene to subtly mislead the reader without lying."

Another powerful technique is to **give the reader the wrong assumptions**. You do this by planting clues, red herrings, or even having characters outright lie. If you show a character sneaking around, arguing with others, and having something to hide, the reader will naturally assume they're up to no good. But maybe they're just trying to protect someone—or maybe they're being blackmailed.

You can also create misperception by showing the story from different **perspectives**. Multiple POV thrillers are great for this because each character has their own limited view of what's happening. They might misunderstand each other's actions, misinterpret evidence, or withhold information.

If you're writing from a single POV, you can still play with perspective by showing how the protagonist's beliefs and emotions color what they see. If your protagonist is paranoid, every innocent action seems like a threat. If they're desperate, they might trust the wrong person. You're filtering the entire story through their lens—and pulling the reader along for the ride.

You can use ChatGPT to help design these perception tricks. Prompt, "How can I use the protagonist's emotional state to mislead the reader in this scene?"

Unreliable narrators are another classic technique. If your protagonist isn't telling the full truth—whether because they're lying, mentally unstable, or hiding something from themselves—it creates a constant question mark in the reader's mind. This isn't just about deception; it's about making the reader question everything they think they know.

A great example is *Gone Girl*, where both main characters manipulate the reader's perception through their unreliable narration. As a writer, you can drop subtle inconsistencies, suspicious gaps in memory, or questionable behavior to make the reader uneasy without revealing the full truth too soon.

ChatGPT can help you craft an unreliable narrator quickly. Ask, "What small details can I include to hint that this narrator might not be telling the full truth?"

Another way to manipulate perception is through **timing and order of information**. You decide when the reader learns something. You can hold back a key piece of information until the midpoint twist. You can show a scene from one character's perspective, then later reveal what was really happening from another character's view.

This is especially useful when you're writing fast. Instead of overcomplicating your plot, you can use the structure itself to mislead the reader and then flip their expectations.

For example, you might open your story with a crime scene and make the reader assume the protagonist is innocent—only to reveal halfway through that they have a dark secret connecting them to the victim.

You can also play with **visual and environmental perception**. Describe a scene in a way that feels one way at first—safe, normal, even boring—and slowly reveal unsettling details that change how the reader sees it. A crowded subway might seem mundane until the protagonist notices the man following them. A friendly dinner might feel warm until the conversation shifts and the tension creeps in.

Atmosphere and description are your tools here. You can ask ChatGPT, "How can I describe this setting to slowly shift the reader's perception from calm to tense?"

Ultimately, what you're doing is making the reader an active participant in the story. They're not just observing; they're trying to solve the puzzle, read between the lines, and figure out what's really going on. And every time you pull the rug out from under them, they'll lean in closer, desperate to see what happens next.

This is what makes thrillers addictive—the feeling that the story is always one step ahead, that nothing can be trusted, that everything is about to shift.

When you're writing your thriller in one day, this is a huge advantage. You don't need to overcomplicate your plot. You can use perception and perspective tricks to make a simple story feel layered and twisty.

The Psychology of Fear and How to Write It

If you strip a thriller down to its core, it's not just about plot twists, ticking clocks, or high-stakes chases. It's about one thing: **fear.** Fear is the fuel that powers every scene, every conflict, every decision your protagonist makes, and every page your reader turns. It's the glue that keeps them glued to the story. So, if you want to write a truly gripping thriller—especially when you're writing it in one day—you need to understand how to tap into the psychology of fear and make your reader feel it.

Let's start with something simple but often overlooked. **Fear is not just about danger.** It's about anticipation. It's not the moment the monster jumps out—it's the moment when the protagonist knows something's about to jump out but doesn't know when. Fear is built in the unknown, the uncertain, the hidden threat that could strike at any second.

Your job as a thriller writer is to stretch that tension as far as it can go without snapping.

One of the best ways to do that is to understand how fear works psychologically. Fear is a survival response. It's triggered when the brain senses a threat, whether physical, emotional, or psychological. And the brain's favorite thing to do in the face of fear? **Fill in the blanks with worst-case scenarios.**

That's why the most terrifying scenes aren't necessarily the ones where something is happening—they're the ones where something **might** happen. When you withhold information, delay the reveal, or hint at danger without showing it, you let the reader's imagination run wild. And trust me, their imagination will always come up with something scarier than anything you can put on the page.

So, how do you write that fear into your thriller?

Start with the **protagonist's internal fears.** What's their worst nightmare? What are they afraid will happen if they fail? Fear doesn't always have to be about physical harm. It can be the fear of losing a loved one, being exposed, losing control, being powerless, or facing the truth about themselves. If you tie the story's external conflict to the protagonist's internal fears, every scene will feel more urgent and more personal.

You can use ChatGPT to help you flesh this out fast. Try prompting, "What is a deep, personal fear that could drive this protagonist in a thriller story?"

Next, use **environment and setting** to amplify the fear. Think about where fear thrives—dark places, confined spaces, abandoned buildings, empty streets, places where help can't reach. But don't stop at the physical. You can create fear through atmosphere: oppressive silence, flickering lights, a sudden drop in temperature, the creak of footsteps behind the protagonist.

Ask ChatGPT, "How can I describe this setting to make it feel eerie and frightening?"

Another technique is to make the protagonist—and the reader—feel **watched.** Being watched is a primal fear. You can create this by having characters sense someone following them, noticing strange behavior, or receiving anonymous messages. When you make your protagonist feel hunted, the reader feels hunted too.

You can also weaponize **uncertainty.** Make the protagonist question what's real and what's not. Is that sound in the hallway just the wind—or is someone there? Is that character really an ally—or are they playing a game? Fear builds in the unknown, so keep your protagonist (and reader) in the dark as long as you can without frustrating them.

When you write, describe the **physical effects of fear**. Shallow breathing. Racing heart. Cold sweat. Tight chest. Tunnel vision. These details pull the reader into the character's experience and make the fear feel real.

You can use ChatGPT to help you write these reactions quickly. Prompt, "Describe a character's physical and emotional reaction to extreme fear."

But here's the thing—fear isn't just for the protagonist. It should be contagious. Your reader should feel fear creeping off the page and into their own chest. You do this by **slowing down key moments.** When something terrifying is about to happen, don't rush. Stretch the moment. Make the reader wait, anticipate, and dread.

A classic technique is the **slow reveal.** Instead of showing the threat immediately, build toward it. Describe the sound first. Then the shadow. Then the glint of something sharp in the dark. Make the reader's skin crawl before the danger even appears.

You can use ChatGPT to help structure these moments. Ask, "How can I build tension in this scene before revealing the threat?"

Another important aspect of writing fear is understanding the difference between **fear and shock.** Shock is what happens when you jump-scare your reader. Fear is what happens when you make them dread what's coming for pages before it arrives. Shock is cheap and fleeting. Fear lingers.

So, don't overuse jump scares or sudden violence. Instead, focus on the slow burn—the rising sense of danger that the protagonist can't escape.

Also, remember that fear can create **irrational behavior.** When people are scared, they make mistakes. They lash out. They freeze. They trust the wrong people. Use this in your story. Put your protagonist under so much pressure that their fear makes them vulnerable.

And don't forget the antagonist. A terrifying villain isn't just physically dangerous—they understand how to use fear. They know how to manipulate, threaten, stalk, and create dread. When your antagonist controls the protagonist's fear, they control the story.

You can use ChatGPT to brainstorm how your villain uses fear. Try prompting, "What psychological tactics could this antagonist use to terrify the protagonist?"

Finally, fear should build toward something. You can't sustain dread forever without a release. That's what the climax is for. All the fear, tension, and anxiety you've built should explode in one final, terrifying confrontation.

When you write your thriller in one day, keep this in mind: You're not just writing events. You're writing a **feeling.** Every scene, every choice, every description should pull the reader deeper into that feeling of dread until they can't stop reading—even when they want to.

Dialogue That Crackles with Suspense

If you want to know what separates an average thriller from a great one, it's often not the action scenes, the car chases, or even the big plot twist at the end. It's the conversations. The tension in a thriller isn't just in what happens—it's in what's **said** and, more importantly, in what's **left unsaid**. Dialogue in a thriller has one job: to crackle with suspense, to keep the reader leaning forward, trying to read between the lines, wondering what every character is really saying.

When you're writing a thriller in one day, you don't have time to write endless exposition or filler chatter. Your dialogue needs to work hard. Every line should either raise the stakes, reveal something hidden, create tension, or flip the story on its head. There's no room for small talk.

So how do you write dialogue that crackles?

The first rule is this: **Dialogue in a thriller is never just dialogue.** It's never casual. It's never just information. Even when two characters are talking about the weather, there should be something beneath the surface—a threat, a lie, a secret. Every conversation should be a chess match.

One of the best ways to create this tension is through **subtext**. Subtext is what's really going on underneath the words. Maybe a character is lying. Maybe they're hiding something. Maybe they're testing the other person. You want the reader to feel like they're eavesdropping on something dangerous or loaded with meaning.

You can use ChatGPT to help you write subtext quickly. Try prompting, "Write tense dialogue between two characters who are pretending to be polite but secretly hate each other."

Another technique is to make your characters speak in **half-truths**. Thriller dialogue works best when characters aren't giving the full story. Let them dodge questions. Change the subject. Say something ambiguous that could mean multiple things. This forces the reader to fill in the blanks—and that's where the suspense lives.

Interruption is another powerful tool. Don't let conversations flow smoothly. People should cut each other off, hesitate, backtrack. Tense conversations are messy because everyone's trying to control the situation. That chaos keeps the reader on edge.

You can also use **short, sharp sentences**. Thriller dialogue isn't about poetic speeches—it's about pressure. Keep the lines snappy. Quick exchanges make the scene feel fast and urgent. When the tension is building, make the sentences shorter. When the characters are trying to manipulate each other, slow it down and make the dialogue more deliberate.

One of the most underrated tricks is using **silence**. Sometimes the most suspenseful part of a conversation is the pause. A character doesn't answer. They hesitate. They let the other person talk too much. Readers feel that gap and wonder why it's there.

Use ChatGPT to help you play with silence. Prompt, "Write a tense dialogue scene where the protagonist's silence makes the antagonist nervous."

Another thing you can do is to build tension with **conflicting agendas**. The best dialogue happens when both characters want different things. One wants information. The other wants to hide something. One wants to confess. The other wants to avoid the truth. When these agendas collide, the conversation becomes a battle—and that's when it crackles.

Questions without answers also keep the tension high. Let your characters ask things that don't get answered immediately. Let them circle each other, testing, probing, but never quite revealing everything. The reader will keep turning pages to get those answers.

You can use ChatGPT to help you craft these moments. Ask, "Write a dialogue scene where one character is trying to get information and the other keeps dodging."

Another way to make your dialogue suspenseful is to let the reader know something the protagonist doesn't. If the reader knows that one character is lying or hiding something, every line of dialogue becomes a ticking bomb. This is where **dramatic irony** comes into play, and it's one of the best ways to inject tension into a conversation.

Think of those great thriller scenes where two characters are sitting across from each other at a table, having what seems like a polite chat—but the reader knows one of them is the killer. Every word is charged because of what the reader knows and the protagonist doesn't.

You can use ChatGPT to help write these kinds of scenes fast. Prompt, "Write a scene where the protagonist is talking to the villain without knowing it."

And don't forget about the **emotional undercurrent**. Fear, anger, suspicion, guilt—all these emotions should be bubbling under the words. If your characters are calm on the surface but cracking underneath, the reader will feel it.

You can also use setting and physical action to amplify the tension. Have characters fidget, avoid eye contact, glance at the door, clench their fists. These little beats between lines of dialogue add to the atmosphere and make the scene feel more alive.

When you're writing fast, one of the best ways to keep your dialogue sharp is to ask yourself:

What does each character want in this scene?

What are they hiding?

What's the tension beneath the words?

If you can answer those questions, you'll write dialogue that isn't just functional—it's electric.

In thrillers, dialogue isn't just about what's said—it's about what's not said. The best lines aren't the ones that explain everything; they're the ones that leave the reader hanging, questioning, dreading what's coming next.

Crafting Short, Sharp Chapters to Control Pacing

One of the most underrated weapons in your thriller-writing toolbox is how you structure your chapters. You can have the best plot twists, the most terrifying villain, and a protagonist worth rooting for—but if your pacing drags, your reader's going to put the book down and go scroll social media. That's why in thrillers, **chapter length and structure are everything**. And the secret sauce is to keep your chapters short, sharp, and always leaving the reader gasping for more.

When you're writing your thriller story in one day, short chapters are your best friend. Not only do they make your book feel fast and addictive, but they also make it easier for you to keep your writing focused, lean, and punchy. You're working against the clock—so writing in tight, contained bursts will help you keep momentum without wandering off into unnecessary subplots or filler.

Let's break down why short chapters work so well in thrillers.

First, they naturally **speed up the pacing**. When a reader sees a chapter that's three pages long instead of thirty, they're much more likely to think, "I've got time for one more." And if you end that short chapter with a cliffhanger, a surprise, or a threat, they'll keep going. Before they know it, it's two in the morning and they've devoured your entire story in one sitting.

Short chapters create a feeling of **urgency**. They mirror the tension in your story. In a thriller, things are always moving fast. The protagonist is racing against the clock. The antagonist is closing in. The danger is building. When your chapters are quick and focused, the reader feels that momentum.

You can use ChatGPT to help you break your story into sharp chapters. Prompt, "Outline how to divide this thriller story into short, suspenseful chapters."

Another reason short chapters are effective is because they give you control over **pacing shifts**. Not every chapter has to be breathless action. Sometimes you want a moment of quiet tension or emotional reflection. By keeping chapters short, you can control exactly how long the reader lingers in each moment. You can speed things up when the action heats up and slow things down when you want to build dread.

Think of short chapters like **beats in a song**. Some are fast and punchy, others are slower and atmospheric—but each one moves the song forward.

Here's how to craft short, sharp chapters that keep the reader hooked:

Start each chapter with a hook.

Don't waste time on scenery or backstory. Drop the reader right into tension, action, or conflict. It could be a new clue, a dangerous confrontation, a secret being revealed. Ask yourself: What's the question or threat driving this chapter?

You can use ChatGPT to help you brainstorm. Prompt, "Give me a strong opening hook for this thriller chapter."

End each chapter with tension.

Leave the reader hanging. A threat, a discovery, a betrayal, a decision left unmade. The best thriller chapters end on cliffhangers—not necessarily life-or-death moments every time, but emotional or narrative hooks that make the reader turn the page.

Ask ChatGPT, "Write a cliffhanger ending for this chapter to keep the reader hooked."

Keep scenes contained.

Each chapter should cover one clear event, encounter, or discovery. Don't let chapters sprawl over multiple locations or time periods. Keep the focus tight. If your protagonist is interrogating a suspect, that's one chapter. If they're breaking into a building, that's another. This keeps the pacing snappy.

Use varied chapter lengths strategically.

While most of your chapters should be short—say, 800 to 1,500 words—you can occasionally break the pattern. A single-page chapter can hit like a punch when you want to deliver a twist or shock. A slightly longer chapter can slow things down when you need an emotional breather.

But in general, the rhythm of short, sharp chapters keeps readers turning pages. It creates a sense of momentum that matches the thriller's tension.

Switch perspectives or locations between chapters.

If your story has multiple POVs, use chapter breaks to jump between them. This adds tension because you can cut away from one character just as something big is happening and drop the reader into another character's equally tense situation. It's the literary equivalent of a TV show cutting to commercial at the worst possible moment.

ChatGPT can help you structure this. Ask, "How can I structure alternating POV chapters to maintain suspense?"

Trim the fat.

Short chapters force you to be economical. There's no room for filler or over-description. Every sentence should serve the story. If a scene or line isn't adding tension, character development, or plot movement, cut it.

When you're writing a thriller in one day, this discipline will help you stay focused. You won't have time to meander—and that's a good thing.

Let your chapters build on each other.

Each chapter should escalate the story. The problem should get worse. The antagonist should get closer. The protagonist should have less time, fewer allies, and more to lose. This stacking effect is what keeps readers glued to the story.

ChatGPT can help you map this escalation. Prompt, "Outline how each chapter can raise the stakes in this thriller story."

Here's an example of how this might look in practice:

Chapter 10: The protagonist discovers a coded message. Chapter 11: They confront their ally, who denies everything. Chapter 12: They break into a location to find the truth. Chapter 13: They're caught—and realize their ally has betrayed them. Chapter 14: They escape, but the antagonist is now one step ahead.

Each chapter is short, direct, and builds on the one before it.

Short chapters also make it easier for you to **track your progress** when writing fast. Instead of thinking, "I need to write 20,000 words today," you can think, "I need to finish the next five chapters." It breaks the work into manageable chunks and keeps you motivated.

How to Write Action and Chase Scenes with ChatGPT

No thriller is complete without that heart-racing moment when everything explodes into action—the chase, the fight, the desperate attempt to escape. These are the moments where your reader stops breathing, where the pages seem to turn themselves. But here's the catch: **writing action and chase scenes is one of the hardest things to get right.** Done poorly, they're confusing, bloated, or boring. Done well, they make your story unforgettable.

When you're writing your thriller in one day, these scenes can feel intimidating because they require energy, choreography, and clarity. But here's the good news—you don't have to do it alone. **ChatGPT is a brilliant partner for writing action and chase scenes quickly, clearly, and cinematically.**

Let's break down how to do it.

First, you need to understand what makes a great action or chase scene work. It's not just about movement—it's about **stakes, tension, and clarity**. Readers need to know who's chasing who, why it matters, and what's at risk. Without that, your scene is just noise.

When you're ready to write an action scene, start by getting clear on three things:

1. **Who's involved?**
2. **What's the goal?**
3. **What's the obstacle?**

For example, your protagonist might be running from the antagonist through a crowded city. The goal is to escape. The obstacle is traffic, pedestrians, and the fact that the antagonist is faster or better prepared.

Once you know the basics, you can use ChatGPT to help you flesh out the details quickly. Start with a simple prompt like, **"Write a fast-paced chase scene where the protagonist is being pursued through a crowded train station."** You'll instantly get a block of descriptive, energetic writing that you can either use directly or tweak to fit your story's voice.

But don't stop there. You can use ChatGPT to make the scene even sharper. Try prompts like:

- "Add sensory details to make the reader feel the protagonist's fear during the chase."
- "Rewrite this scene with shorter sentences to increase tension."
- "Describe how the protagonist uses the environment to evade capture."

These micro-prompts are your secret weapon when you're racing to write your thriller in one day. You can build the skeleton of the action scene fast and then refine it with specific prompts to sharpen the pacing and tension.

Let's talk about **clarity**. One of the biggest mistakes writers make in action scenes is overcomplicating the choreography. If readers can't picture who's where, what's happening, or why it matters, they'll get confused and tune out. You want your scene to feel cinematic, like the reader is watching it play out shot by shot.

To do this, focus on **one clear action per sentence**. Keep sentences short and sharp. Use active verbs. Cut unnecessary description. Think in beats:

- He ducks.
- She lunges.
- Tires screech.
- Footsteps pound behind him.

You can even prompt ChatGPT, **"Rewrite this action scene with clear, simple sentences."** This will help you strip out the clutter and keep the reader locked in the moment.

Pacing matters too. A long paragraph slows the scene down. Break up the action with short paragraphs, even single lines. This creates white space on the page and makes the reader's eyes move faster—mirroring the speed and chaos of the chase.

Here's another trick: **cut the internal monologue.** During an action or chase scene, you want the protagonist focused on survival, not reflecting on their childhood trauma. Save introspection for after the danger passes. Keep the scene in the present moment. Every thought should be about the immediate danger.

That said, a sprinkle of **fear or panic** inside the protagonist's head can heighten the tension—just keep it brief and urgent. You can ask ChatGPT, **"Add a few internal thoughts showing the protagonist's fear without slowing the scene."**

Another way ChatGPT can help you is by brainstorming **environmental obstacles**. You can prompt, **"What obstacles could a protagonist face during a foot chase through a warehouse?"** You'll get a list of ideas you can drop right into your scene—slippery floors, stacked crates, faulty lighting, unexpected dead ends.

Vary the chase. Don't make it a straight-line sprint. Have the protagonist scramble through a market, duck into alleys, climb over fences, or jump between rooftops. The more the environment interacts with the chase, the more thrilling and unpredictable it feels.

You can also use ChatGPT to add these details quickly. Prompt, **"Describe how the protagonist evades capture by using the environment creatively."**

And don't forget to end the scene with a **payoff**. A chase scene shouldn't just fizzle out. Either the protagonist escapes, gets caught, or something unexpected happens—like discovering a clue in the chaos. You can use ChatGPT to help brainstorm strong endings: **"Give me three possible ways this chase scene could end with a twist."**

Here's a quick example workflow you can use when writing fast:

1. Outline who's chasing who, why, and where.
2. Use ChatGPT to generate an action scene draft.
3. Prompt ChatGPT to sharpen the pacing, add sensory details, and simplify sentence structure.
4. Rewrite or edit for your protagonist's voice.
5. End with a clear resolution or cliffhanger.

Action and chase scenes are the adrenaline spikes of your thriller. They give the reader that rush, that sense of danger and movement. But they only work if you balance clarity with tension and speed with stakes. When you're writing a thriller in one day, ChatGPT can help you craft these scenes quickly and cleanly, without sacrificing quality.

In the next chapter, we'll talk about how to use **internal monologue and character thoughts** to pull the reader deeper into the protagonist's fear, doubt, and emotional turmoil—without slowing down the pacing.

Internal Monologue – Letting the Reader inside the Protagonist's Mind

If there's one thing that makes a thriller story stick in a reader's mind long after they've finished it, it's not just the plot twists or chase scenes—it's the experience of being inside the protagonist's head. It's feeling their fear, doubt, suspicion, rage, and panic as if it were your own. That's what internal monologue does. It pulls the reader so close to the protagonist that every danger, betrayal, and threat feels personal. And when you're writing your thriller in one day, learning how to use internal monologue properly can elevate your story fast without slowing you down.

But let's get something clear: **internal monologue is not the same as endless exposition or backstory.** It's not about your character sitting around thinking deeply about the meaning of life while the antagonist closes in. In a thriller, internal monologue is all about tension, reaction, and emotional immediacy.

It's your chance to show the reader how the protagonist is processing what's happening—what they fear, what they suspect, what they want to do next, and what they're hiding even from themselves.

So how do you use it without slowing down your pacing or losing the reader in a sea of thoughts?

Start by understanding that internal monologue in a thriller should be **short, sharp, and emotionally charged**. You're not writing a reflective novel about self-discovery—you're writing a story where your protagonist is in constant danger. Their thoughts should reflect that.

Instead of long paragraphs of reflection, give the reader **snapshots** of what's happening inside the protagonist's mind. One or two lines between actions. A single, cutting observation. A flash of doubt or panic.

For example:

She glanced over her shoulder. No sign of him. Yet.

Maybe I've lost him.

Or maybe he's waiting around the next corner.

That's internal monologue that works. It's quick. It's tense. It keeps the reader in the protagonist's head without slowing down the scene.

When you're writing fast, ChatGPT can help you add this layer easily. Prompt, **"Add short, tense internal monologue to this scene showing the protagonist's fear and doubt."** You'll get ready-to-drop-in thoughts that match the pace of the action.

Another thing to remember is that internal monologue is your secret weapon for building **suspense**. Readers can't always see the protagonist's facial expressions or body language in a book. Internal thoughts give them access to what's **really** going on.

For example, in a tense conversation with a possible traitor, your protagonist might smile and nod on the outside—but inside, their thoughts are spinning:

He's lying. I can see it in his eyes.

But why? What's he hiding?

Stay calm. Don't let him see you know.

You can even use internal monologue to **mislead the reader**—especially if you're writing from a first-person or deep third-person perspective. Maybe the protagonist is wrong about something. Maybe they're paranoid. Maybe they're lying to themselves. Their internal thoughts can reflect that and keep the reader guessing.

You can ask ChatGPT, **"Write an unreliable internal monologue for this protagonist who suspects everyone around them."** This helps you plant seeds of doubt without giving away your twists too early.

Another thing internal monologue is great for is showing the protagonist's **emotional arc**. In a thriller, your protagonist is under constant pressure. They're scared, desperate, angry, broken. But they're also fighting back. You can use their thoughts to show how they're changing over the course of the story.

At the start, their internal monologue might be filled with fear and confusion:

I can't do this. I'm not strong enough.

I don't even know what's going on.

But by the climax, their thoughts should reflect how much they've grown:

I've come this far. I'm not running anymore.

If he wants to end this, he'll have to go through me.

That's character development—delivered straight from the protagonist's mind.

Pacing is key. In fast action scenes, keep internal thoughts brief. Let them interrupt the action, but not slow it down. In quieter, tension-building scenes, you can go a little deeper and let the protagonist's doubts and fears spill out more.

You can also use internal monologue to clarify the protagonist's **choices**. Sometimes in thrillers, readers wonder why the protagonist made a risky or seemingly foolish decision. Internal thoughts can show the reasoning, the desperation, or the emotional trigger behind those choices.

For example:

I could wait for backup.

But by then, she'll be dead.

That one line gives the reader everything they need to understand why the protagonist is about to break the rules.

When you're writing your thriller in one day, internal monologue is a tool you can use **on the fly** to add depth and tension without rewriting entire scenes. You can use ChatGPT as a writing partner here.

Try prompts like:

- **"What would the protagonist be thinking in this scene?"**
- **"Add internal monologue showing the protagonist's growing paranoia."**

- **"Rewrite this paragraph to include the protagonist's fear and doubt."**

These prompts will help you layer in tension and character emotion as you write, without losing momentum.

And here's a bonus: internal monologue is also a great place to plant clues and foreshadowing. Maybe your protagonist keeps thinking about a detail that seems minor—but later turns out to be crucial. Or maybe they dismiss a hunch that ends up being right. Readers will remember those thoughts, even if the protagonist doesn't.

Just remember: **Keep it short. Keep it sharp. Keep it emotional.** Internal monologue should feel like a heartbeat pulsing under every scene, pulling the reader closer to the protagonist's experience.

Building Emotional Tension in Quiet Moments

When people think of thrillers, they usually picture car chases, explosions, and jaw-dropping plot twists. But the truth is, some of the most powerful, suspenseful, and unforgettable moments in a thriller don't happen when things are loud and fast—they happen in the **quiet moments**. It's in the silence between the action that the real tension builds. It's when your protagonist is alone, doubting, questioning, or confronting something personal and terrifying that the story tightens its grip on the reader's throat.

If you want your thriller to hit hard and leave a mark, you need to learn how to master these quiet moments and fill them with **emotional tension**. And when you're writing your thriller in one day, knowing how to use these scenes strategically will help you give your reader a breather without letting them relax.

So, what exactly do we mean by "quiet moments"?

Quiet moments are the **spaces between the chaos**. They're when your protagonist is driving home after a confrontation. When they're sitting alone in their apartment, staring at a wall, piecing together clues. When they're having a tense conversation over coffee with someone they're not sure they can trust. No guns blazing, no explosions—just an undercurrent of dread, fear, doubt, or longing.

These scenes are essential because they allow the reader to catch their breath—but not to feel safe. They create a slow-burn tension that keeps the suspense alive, even when nothing is happening on the surface.

So how do you build emotional tension in these moments?

The first key is to focus on the **protagonist's emotional state**. After a big action scene or plot twist, your protagonist isn't just moving to the next location. They're processing. They're hurting. They're afraid, or guilty, or angry, or determined. These emotions should simmer beneath every quiet scene.

Instead of having your protagonist simply sit and think, let their emotions **leak out** into their behavior, their dialogue, and their internal monologue. Maybe they can't sit still. Maybe they obsessively re-read a piece of evidence. Maybe they snap at an ally who's only trying to help.

You can use ChatGPT to help you layer this in quickly. Prompt, **"Describe the protagonist's emotional tension after a near-death experience."** You'll get ready-made lines that capture that uneasy, simmering energy.

Another way to build tension is to use **subtext in dialogue**. In quiet scenes, what's being said isn't nearly as important as what's not being said. Two characters might be talking about the case—but underneath, they're really accusing, distrusting, or testing each other. The tension comes from what's left unsaid, from the emotions hiding between the lines.

Ask ChatGPT, **"Write a tense, quiet dialogue scene where two characters talk about the case but are really talking about their broken trust."**

Setting can also amplify emotional tension in quiet moments. A quiet apartment after a break-in. An empty street late at night. A hospital waiting room. These places feel heavy when paired with the right emotional undercurrent. They reflect the protagonist's isolation, fear, or inner turmoil.

You can prompt ChatGPT, **"Describe a setting that feels emotionally tense and lonely for the protagonist."**

Another trick is to use **small physical details** to reflect the tension. A character tapping their foot. A hand tightening into a fist. A glance that lingers too long. These subtle cues show the reader that something is wrong, even if the characters are pretending everything is fine.

You can even use **sound and silence** as tools. The ticking of a clock. A distant siren. The hum of a refrigerator. These sounds become oppressive when everything else is quiet, making the reader feel like something's about to snap.

Internal monologue also plays a big role here. In quiet scenes, you can let the protagonist's thoughts spiral—second-guessing themselves, reliving traumatic moments, fearing what's coming next. But keep it sharp and tense. No meandering reflection—just the raw, anxious voice of someone who knows the worst is still ahead.

One of the most effective uses of quiet moments is to show your protagonist's **vulnerability**. In the chaos of a thriller, your protagonist is usually fighting, running, surviving. But in the quiet, they're exposed. That's when the reader sees their flaws, their fears, their breaking point. And that's what makes the reader care.

You can ask ChatGPT, **"Write an internal monologue showing the protagonist's vulnerability after a major loss."**

Don't underestimate the power of a quiet scene right before or after a big twist or action sequence. These are called **breather scenes**, but they're not a chance for the reader to relax—they're a chance to twist the emotional knife.

For example, after a big chase scene, you might have a chapter where the protagonist returns home, alone, realizing how close they came to dying—and how few people they can trust. That's emotional tension that lingers.

Or before a major confrontation, you might give the protagonist a quiet scene where they hesitate, question their choices, and almost break. This isn't wasted space—it's the buildup that makes the next explosion hit harder.

When you're writing your thriller fast, you can use ChatGPT to structure these moments efficiently. Try prompting:

- **"Write a quiet, tense scene that shows the protagonist's emotional exhaustion."**
- **"What emotional conflict can I show in this scene without slowing the pace?"**
- **"How can I use setting and small details to create tension in a quiet moment?"**

The key is to remember that tension isn't just about action. It's about what the protagonist feels when everything slows down. It's about the reader knowing that danger is still out there, even when the scene is quiet.

If you master emotional tension in these moments, your thriller won't just be fast-paced—it will be layered, gripping, and unforgettable.

Incorporating Mystery Elements without Losing Momentum

Thrillers and mysteries often get bundled together on bookstore shelves—and for good reason. They share a lot of the same DNA: secrets, questions, shocking twists, and a protagonist digging deeper into dangerous territory. But here's something important to understand when you're writing a thriller, especially when you're writing it fast in one day. A **thriller is about tension and danger; a mystery is about questions and answers.** Your challenge is to sprinkle mystery elements into your thriller without slowing down the action or losing that relentless forward momentum.

The key is balance. You want your reader to be asking questions, but you don't want them stuck in exposition or bogged down in detective work. Thrillers should feel like a ticking time bomb—not a quiet night in a detective's office connecting red string on a corkboard.

So, how do you weave mystery into your thriller without killing the pace?

The first rule is to let the **mystery drive the action.** In a mystery novel, the protagonist usually investigates after the fact. In a thriller, the mystery should unfold **while the protagonist is being hunted, running, or fighting back.** The questions and puzzles should fuel the tension, not pause it.

Think of it like this: In a mystery, the protagonist is chasing the truth. In a thriller, the truth is chasing them.

When you're outlining or drafting, use ChatGPT to help you blend these threads together. Prompt, **"How can I tie the central mystery into the protagonist's immediate danger in this thriller?"**

One of the simplest and most effective ways to incorporate mystery is to make sure your protagonist is always working with **incomplete information.** Don't give them (or the reader) the full picture. They should constantly be one step behind the antagonist, questioning who to trust, what's really happening, and what's waiting around the next corner.

You can use ChatGPT to generate these gaps. Ask, **"What crucial piece of information can I withhold from the protagonist to keep the mystery alive?"**

Another great technique is to drop **breadcrumbs** throughout the story—clues, hints, pieces of evidence. But instead of stopping the story to explain them, let the protagonist (and the reader) gather them **on the run.** Maybe they notice something strange during a fight. Maybe they overhear a key piece of information while escaping. The mystery should feel like something that's being uncovered **under pressure.**

You can prompt ChatGPT, **"Suggest subtle clues I can drop in fast-paced thriller scenes."**

Red herrings also work beautifully in a thriller. These are false leads or clues designed to mislead both the protagonist and the reader. But the trick is to reveal them naturally in the middle of tense scenes—not in long, boring exposition. A suspicious character who turns out to be innocent. A clue that points to the wrong suspect. A conversation that seems to reveal everything but is really a lie.

Mystery also thrives in **character behavior.** Make your supporting characters behave suspiciously. Have them hide things, contradict themselves, or show signs they're not telling the whole truth. The protagonist should constantly be asking, **Who can I trust?** And the reader should be asking the same thing.

One easy way to do this is to use ChatGPT to generate dialogue with subtext. Try prompting, **"Write a tense conversation where one character is hiding something from the protagonist."**

Another way to weave mystery in without slowing things down is to use **layered reveals.** Don't dump all the answers at once. Each time the protagonist solves one piece of the puzzle, it should raise two more questions. The mystery unfolds alongside the action, keeping the reader guessing and the story moving forward.

You can even use ChatGPT to help structure these reveals. Ask, **"Outline how I can reveal clues and twists gradually in this thriller."**

A mistake many thriller writers make is spending too much time explaining the mystery. Readers don't need a full investigation scene after every clue. Let the protagonist figure things out **in motion**—while being chased, fighting, or on the run. Keep the tension high while they piece together the answers.

Also, don't forget to tie the mystery to the protagonist's **personal stakes.** The best thrillers aren't just about what's happening—they're about why it matters to the protagonist. The mystery isn't an intellectual exercise. It's life or death. If the protagonist doesn't solve it, they lose everything.

Use ChatGPT to help clarify this connection. Prompt, **"How can I connect the central mystery to the protagonist's personal stakes?"**

And finally, always remember to deliver a satisfying resolution. Readers will forgive all kinds of red herrings and unanswered questions during the story—but by the end, they want the truth. Make sure you reveal the mystery clearly and cleanly during your climax, without slowing down the final confrontation.

A good thriller mystery ending isn't a long speech—it's a sharp reveal that hits the protagonist like a punch in the gut, usually in the middle of a confrontation, a chase, or a fight.

When you're writing your thriller in one day, mystery elements are a brilliant way to **layer tension, deepen character conflict, and keep the reader guessing**. But don't let them clog the story with overcomplicated investigation scenes. Keep the mystery embedded in the action.

How to Write Gripping Cliffhangers Every Chapter

If there's one tool that can keep your reader locked into your thriller, eyes wide, flipping page after page long after they promised themselves, "Just one more chapter"—it's the **cliffhanger**. A good cliffhanger is the heartbeat of thriller storytelling. It's what makes the reader lean forward and think, "I can't stop now. I have to know what happens next." And when you're writing your thriller in one day, mastering the art of chapter-ending cliffhangers is how you keep that momentum going strong from start to finish.

The first thing to understand is that a cliffhanger doesn't always mean a character dangling off a literal cliff. A cliffhanger is any kind of **unresolved tension** or **shocking revelation** that makes the reader desperate to keep going. It's the story equivalent of a loaded gun on the table that's about to go off—but you cut the scene right before it does.

So how do you craft these addictive endings chapter after chapter without making them feel repetitive or forced?

Start by recognizing that there are different **types of cliffhangers** you can use. Let's look at a few:

1. The Threat Cliffhanger

This is the classic. End the chapter at the moment of immediate danger. A gun pointed at the protagonist. A door creaking open in the dark. A villain stepping out of the shadows. You stop the chapter right when things are about to explode.

2. The Revelation Cliffhanger

Instead of physical danger, end the chapter on a shocking piece of information. A secret uncovered. A betrayal revealed. A clue that changes everything. The kind of twist that makes the reader gasp and need to know what's next.

3. The Emotional Cliffhanger

Sometimes the tension isn't external—it's emotional. End the chapter on a moment of heartbreak, anger, or fear. Maybe the protagonist discovers they've been lied to by someone they love. Maybe they realize they've made a terrible mistake.

4. The Decision Cliffhanger

This is when you end the chapter right before the protagonist makes a crucial choice. Do they pull the trigger? Do they walk away? Do they trust the person across the table? The reader has to keep going to find out.

5. The Misdirection Cliffhanger

End on a line or image that hints at something shocking—but the next chapter flips it. Maybe you end with the protagonist seeing a gun in someone's hand, but the next chapter reveals they were just cleaning it. This keeps readers second-guessing everything.

You can use ChatGPT to help you come up with these quickly when you're writing fast. Prompt, **"Suggest a strong cliffhanger ending for this chapter based on the protagonist's current situation."**

The trick to writing great cliffhangers is to **leave the reader hanging—but not confused**. You want them desperate to know what happens, not frustrated by a lack of information. A cliffhanger isn't about withholding everything. It's about stopping at the perfect moment, when the tension is at its highest.

Think of it like this: Every chapter should end on a sharp **question** in the reader's mind. Will the protagonist survive? What does that clue mean? Who can be trusted? You don't have to answer right away—but you have to make the reader want the answer so badly that they turn the page.

Another key is to make sure your cliffhangers aren't empty shocks. They should **matter** to the story and the protagonist. If you end every chapter with a car crash, but none of them have real consequences, the reader will stop caring. Your cliffhangers should escalate the stakes, deepen the mystery, or hit the protagonist where it hurts.

When you're writing fast, you can use a simple formula to check if your cliffhanger is strong enough:

1. Is there unresolved tension?
2. Does it raise a question in the reader's mind?
3. Does it make the protagonist's situation worse, scarier, or more uncertain?

If the answer is yes, you've got a solid chapter ending.

Here's another pro tip: **Vary your cliffhangers.** Don't end every chapter with a gun to the head or a literal explosion. Mix it up. Sometimes end on a shocking piece of information. Sometimes end on a quiet, ominous line. Sometimes end on the protagonist's realization that they're in deeper trouble than they thought.

You can use ChatGPT to help you brainstorm different types of cliffhangers. Ask, **"Give me three different cliffhanger options for this chapter: one physical threat, one emotional shock, and one revelation."**

One of the best ways to keep your reader hooked is to chain your cliffhangers together. Each chapter ending should set up the next scene's conflict. The tension should snowball. If your protagonist barely escapes danger in one chapter, the next chapter should open with a new threat already closing in. Think of your cliffhangers like stepping stones across a river. Each one keeps the reader moving forward, never giving them a safe place to stop.

And don't forget that you can use cliffhangers at the end of **acts** as well as chapters. These are the big turning points in your story—the midpoint twist, the dark moment before the climax. Make sure these cliffhangers are even bigger, hitting hard emotionally and narratively.

When you're writing your thriller in one day, cliffhangers are your best tool to keep the pacing tight and the reader hooked. But here's the final secret: your cliffhangers will only work if you **pay them off**. Don't tease danger or mystery and never deliver. When you end a chapter on a question, make sure you answer it—just in time to raise another.

Writing the Protagonist's Personal Stakes

If you want your thriller to be more than just a series of fast-paced events, if you want it to linger in the reader's mind and make them care deeply about what happens, you need to understand one thing: **personal stakes**. The chases, the twists, the cliffhangers—they're all fun, but they don't mean a thing if the reader doesn't care what your protagonist stands to lose.

Personal stakes are the difference between a thriller that's just entertaining and one that's gripping, gut-wrenching, and unforgettable.

When we talk about "stakes" in storytelling, we're talking about what's at risk. But in a thriller, there are usually two layers: the **external stakes** (stop the killer, prevent the bomb from going off, expose the conspiracy) and the **internal, personal stakes**. These are the things that hit your protagonist in the heart. Their family, their freedom, their reputation, their sanity, their soul.

It's the personal stakes that will make your reader stay up all night.

When you're writing your thriller in one day, you might be tempted to focus entirely on the external stakes because they're easier to plot. But if you spend just a little time early in your outline nailing down the protagonist's personal stakes, the writing will flow faster, the tension will feel real, and your story will pack a much bigger punch.

So, how do you do that?

First, ask yourself: **Why does this story matter to my protagonist personally?**

Why is this more than just another case, another job, another day in the life? What will they lose if they fail—not just globally, but intimately?

Maybe your protagonist's personal stake is their family. If they don't solve the mystery, their spouse or child is in danger. Maybe it's their own freedom—if they fail, they'll be framed, imprisoned, or killed. Maybe it's their reputation—the truth they're chasing could destroy them. Or maybe it's something more internal—their sanity, their sense of self, their chance at redemption.

Whatever it is, it has to matter deeply to them. It has to hurt.

You can use ChatGPT to help you flesh this out quickly. Prompt, **"What personal stakes could this protagonist have in a thriller about [insert plot]?"** You'll get a list of emotional, intimate risks you can weave into your story.

Once you know your protagonist's personal stakes, the next step is to make sure those stakes are **visible and urgent** throughout the story. Don't just mention them once at the beginning and forget about them. Remind the reader of what's on the line at every turn.

For example, if the protagonist's child has been kidnapped, don't let the reader forget it. Show the protagonist glancing at a photo on their phone during a tense scene. Let their thoughts flicker to the promise they made to bring their child home. If the protagonist is facing public ruin, show them checking their phone for news reports, haunted by headlines that haven't been written yet.

The stakes need to **haunt** your protagonist. They need to weigh on every decision, every mistake, every risk they take.

You can use ChatGPT to help you thread these reminders into your scenes. Ask, **"How can I show the protagonist's personal stakes during this action scene without slowing the pace?"**

Another powerful technique is to make sure the personal stakes **escalate** alongside the external stakes. As the protagonist gets closer to the truth, the danger to their personal world should get worse. Maybe they're being framed and the evidence against them keeps piling up. Maybe their loved ones start to question them or pull away. Maybe they're pushed closer and closer to becoming the thing they hate.

The closer the protagonist gets to solving the external conflict, the more their personal stakes should be under threat. That's what creates real tension.

And don't forget: your antagonist can (and should) exploit the protagonist's personal stakes. If your villain knows what matters most to the protagonist, they'll use it. They'll threaten their family. They'll dangle their freedom like bait. They'll force the protagonist into impossible choices.

You can ask ChatGPT to help you plot these emotional attacks. Prompt, **"How can the antagonist threaten the protagonist's personal stakes in this thriller?"**

One more thing—your protagonist's personal stakes should also tie into their **character arc**. Maybe they start the story thinking the mission is just about justice, but they realize it's really about protecting someone they love. Maybe they believe they're doing the right thing, but their personal stake forces them to question their morality.

By the end of the story, your protagonist should have changed—not just because they stopped the bad guy, but because the fight cost them something personal. That's what makes a thriller resonate. The external conflict is exciting, but the internal cost is what makes it unforgettable.

When you're writing your thriller quickly, it's easy to focus on the big picture—the plot, the twists, the danger. But if you take the time to build your protagonist's personal stakes into every scene, you'll write a story that keeps readers not only turning pages, but **feeling something**.

Foreshadowing and Callbacks – How to Tie Your Story Together

One of the best feelings as a thriller reader is when you hit the climax of the story and suddenly everything clicks. That little clue in chapter three. That weird line of dialogue in chapter seven. That minor character who seemed irrelevant. All of it snaps into place and you realize the writer had been setting the trap the whole time. That's the magic of **foreshadowing** and **callbacks**—and if you want your thriller to feel tight, polished, and cleverly constructed (even when you've written it in one day), you need to master how to use them.

First, let's talk about **foreshadowing**. Foreshadowing is the art of planting seeds early in your story that hint at what's coming later. It creates a sense of inevitability and cohesion. Done well, it makes your reader gasp and think, "Of course! I should've seen that coming." Done poorly—or not at all—and your twists can feel cheap or random.

But here's the trick: in a thriller, foreshadowing should be subtle. You don't want to wave a neon sign that says, **This Will Be Important Later**. You want to slide in details, lines of dialogue, background clues that seem minor at first but take on huge meaning by the end.

For example, maybe in the first act, your protagonist notices a broken security camera while walking past a building. No big deal. But later, when they're trying to piece together a timeline, that broken camera is the key to everything. Or maybe a side character mentions an old grudge in passing—only to reveal themselves as the real threat in the climax.

When you're writing fast, you can use ChatGPT to help you plant these seeds efficiently. Prompt, **"What small details can I include early in this thriller that will pay off later?"** You'll get ideas you can scatter throughout your early chapters.

The easiest way to structure foreshadowing is to tie it to your major plot twists. Think about the big reveals you have planned and ask yourself: **How can I hint at this earlier without giving it away?** Maybe it's a piece of evidence that seems irrelevant. Maybe it's something the antagonist says offhandedly. Maybe it's a gut feeling the protagonist ignores.

You can even foreshadow emotional turns. If your protagonist is going to make a huge personal sacrifice at the climax, sprinkle in moments early on that show what matters most to them—or that show how far they're willing to go.

Now let's talk about **callbacks**. A callback is when you reference something that happened earlier in the story—an event, a line of dialogue, a decision—and give it new meaning. This is how you reward attentive readers and tie your story together in a satisfying way.

For example, maybe in chapter two, your protagonist tells a friend, **"I don't run from a fight."** In the final act, when they're faced with impossible odds, that line echoes back in their mind as they choose to stand their ground. That's a callback. It's not a plot twist, but it adds weight and emotional payoff to the story.

Or maybe you have a recurring image or phrase that pops up at key moments—like the sound of a ticking clock whenever time is running out. That's a callback, and it creates cohesion and rhythm in your thriller.

You can use ChatGPT to help you brainstorm callbacks as you write. Try prompting, **"What early scene or line could I reference in the climax of this thriller to give it emotional weight?"**

One thing to keep in mind is that foreshadowing and callbacks work best when they feel **organic**. They shouldn't feel like the writer is showing off how clever they are. They should feel like the natural result of the protagonist's journey and the events of the story.

When you're writing your thriller in one day, here's a practical workflow:

1. As you outline or draft, jot down a few major twists and emotional beats.
2. Ask yourself, **What little hints can I plant early to set this up?**
3. As you write, drop in those details casually—no big explanation.
4. When you reach the midpoint and climax, circle back to those earlier moments. Let the reader connect the dots and feel that satisfying "aha" moment.

Foreshadowing isn't just about plot twists. It also builds **tension**. When you subtly hint at danger early on, the reader feels it without knowing why. It creates a thread of unease that keeps them turning pages.

Callbacks, on the other hand, give the story emotional and narrative closure. They make the reader feel like everything mattered—that every line, every clue, every moment led to this.

A thriller without foreshadowing and callbacks can still be exciting—but it won't feel as **tight** or as **rewarding**. These are the tools that tie everything together and make your story feel like a brilliantly constructed puzzle.

And here's the beauty of it: You don't have to spend days laboring over this. You can use ChatGPT to help you identify opportunities for foreshadowing and callbacks as you write. Prompt, **"Suggest ways to foreshadow the antagonist's betrayal early in the story."** Or, **"What moment from Act One can I reference in the climax for emotional impact?"**

The more you use these techniques, the more professional and satisfying your thriller will feel—even if you wrote the whole thing in a day.

The Role of Lies, Secrets, and Betrayals

If there's one thing that keeps thriller readers hooked, page after page, it's the simple but powerful question: **Who can I trust?** That question is the heartbeat of every great thriller. And the reason it works so well is because thrillers thrive on a web of **lies, secrets, and betrayals.** These elements aren't just juicy plot points—they're the fuel that keeps the tension burning and the reader questioning everything they thought they knew.

When you're writing a thriller in one day, this is one of the fastest and most effective ways to inject layers into your story without overcomplicating it. You don't need a massive cast of characters or an intricate conspiracy to pull this off. You just need to know how to plant and reveal the right lies, secrets, and betrayals at the right time.

Let's break down why these elements are so essential—and how to use them properly.

Lies are the currency of thrillers. Characters lie to each other constantly—for good reasons, bad reasons, or reasons they don't even understand themselves. Your protagonist lies to protect themselves or others. The antagonist lies to manipulate and control. Supporting characters lie because they're scared, hiding something, or trying to survive.

The key is to make sure the lies have **consequences**. A lie isn't just thrown into the story to be forgotten—it should ripple outward, affecting the plot and character relationships. Maybe the protagonist lies to an ally to keep them safe, only for that lie to backfire later. Maybe a minor character lies about something small, but that lie hides something much bigger.

You can use ChatGPT to help you design these lies on the fly. Prompt, **"What lie could the protagonist tell in this scene that will come back to haunt them later?"**

Secrets are closely tied to lies but slightly different. A lie is an active deception. A secret is something hidden—whether deliberately or not. In a thriller, everyone has secrets. The protagonist. The antagonist. The side characters. And every time a secret is revealed, it should shake the foundation of what the reader and protagonist believe to be true.

The best thriller secrets are the ones that change the story's direction when uncovered. Maybe the protagonist discovers that their trusted ally has a connection to the antagonist. Maybe the antagonist is hiding a personal motive that flips the reader's understanding of the story. Maybe the protagonist is keeping a dark secret from their own past that affects everything they do.

When you're writing fast, you can use ChatGPT to brainstorm secrets quickly. Try, **"What secret could this character be hiding that, when revealed, will change the story?"**

Betrayal is the payoff of lies and secrets. It's the moment when the truth comes out—and it hurts. Betrayal is what makes the reader gasp, what makes the protagonist question everything, what shatters alliances and forces them to fight harder.

A betrayal in a thriller shouldn't come out of nowhere. It should feel shocking, but when the reader looks back, they should realize the clues were there all along. That's why lies and secrets work best when they're planted early and revealed at the worst possible moment.

You can use ChatGPT to help you structure this. Prompt, **"Outline a betrayal reveal in this thriller that flips the story and raises the stakes."**

One important thing to remember is that not all betrayals have to be huge or life-threatening. Sometimes the most painful betrayals are personal. A friend who lies. A loved one who keeps a secret. A colleague who chooses their own safety over the protagonist's. These moments create emotional tension that's just as gripping as physical danger.

When you're writing your thriller quickly, you can use a simple structure to weave lies, secrets, and betrayals into your story:

1. **Decide early on what each key character is hiding.** Even your protagonist.
2. **Drop hints without revealing the full truth.** Let characters act suspicious, contradict themselves, or avoid certain topics.
3. **Let the protagonist's choices be shaped by what they think they know—and by the lies they've been told.**
4. **Reveal the truth at the worst possible moment.** Midpoint twist. Climax. A moment when the protagonist thinks they've won—only to realize everything they believed was a lie.

Here's an example:

In the first act, the protagonist's closest ally tells them they've never met the antagonist. You, as the writer, know that's a lie. The reader doesn't. Throughout the story, you drop little hints—an offhand comment, a hesitation, a photo in the background. In the second act, the protagonist discovers the truth: the ally used to work with the antagonist. Betrayal. Tension explodes.

This kind of reveal is easy to structure when you're writing fast because you can plan it upfront, then plant small clues as you go. You don't need a hundred secrets. Two or three well-placed lies and one or two devastating betrayals are more than enough to make your thriller hit hard.

And here's one more thing: **Let your protagonist lie, too.** Readers love flawed heroes. If your protagonist hides something, protects themselves with lies, or even betrays someone for what they think is the greater good, it adds complexity and makes the story more unpredictable.

When you're writing your thriller in one day, you can use ChatGPT to help you keep track of who's lying to whom. Prompt, **"Create a list of character lies and secrets for this thriller story."** This will help you stay organized and make sure you pay off each reveal.

How to Handle Violence and Threat in a Thriller

Let's be honest—thrillers are built on the edge of violence. It's the shadow that hangs over every conversation, every chase, every twist. But violence in a thriller isn't about gore or body count. It's about **threat**. It's about how close the protagonist comes to danger and how that danger shapes the tension of the story. And when you're writing your thriller in one day, knowing how to handle violence and threat without overdoing it—or undercutting your story—is a skill you need to master.

The first thing to understand is that **threat is more powerful than violence itself.** Readers feel fear and tension not when a gun goes off, but when they're waiting for it to go off. The anticipation of violence is where the real suspense lives.

That's why you don't have to fill your thriller with non-stop shootouts, fistfights, or gruesome scenes. What you need is the constant, simmering presence of danger. The sense that something could snap at any second.

When you're writing fast, this is actually good news. You don't need to waste time choreographing endless action scenes. You need to master how to **imply violence**, how to make the reader feel it looming without always showing it.

You can do this with **setting, atmosphere, and character behavior.** The alley that's too quiet. The antagonist who smiles too much. The weapon resting casually on a table. These details create a world where violence feels like it could erupt at any moment.

You can use ChatGPT to help you paint this tension quickly. Prompt, **"Describe a setting that feels threatening without actual violence."**

That said, when you do decide to show violence, it should always be **purposeful.** Violence in a thriller should never be random or gratuitous. It should escalate the stakes, reveal something about the characters, or force a turning point in the plot.

For example, a sudden act of violence might show how far the antagonist is willing to go—or how far the protagonist is willing to go when pushed. It might mark the moment when the protagonist crosses a line they can't uncross.

Ask yourself every time you write a violent moment: **What is the story cost?**

Who gets hurt? What changes? What choice does this force the protagonist to make?

You can use ChatGPT to help you sharpen this. Prompt, **"How can this violent moment in my thriller change the protagonist's situation?"**

Restraint is another important part of handling violence. You don't need to describe every broken bone or bloody detail. In fact, less is often more. A sharp, clinical description can hit harder than a long, gory paragraph. Focus on how the violence feels—emotionally and physically—to the protagonist.

Here's an example:

Instead of writing:

The knife slashed across his arm, skin tearing open, blood gushing down.

You can write:

A burning line across his arm, sharp and fast. He didn't even realize he'd been cut until the blood warmed his fingers.

The violence is there, but it's lean, focused, visceral. It makes the reader **feel it** without wallowing in it.

When you're writing fast, this also keeps your pacing tight. Violence in a thriller should be like a slap—quick, shocking, and leaving an echo.

Another important aspect is how characters **respond to violence.** No one walks away from violence unchanged. Whether it's a fight, a shooting, or a near-death escape, the aftermath matters.

Let your protagonist carry the scars—physical, emotional, or both. Let them shake, bleed, break down. Readers want to see the consequences, not just the action. And those consequences build tension for the next threat.

You can use ChatGPT to help you show this. Ask, **"Describe the protagonist's emotional and physical reaction after a violent encounter."**

Also, think about how violence can change **relationships** in your story. Maybe the protagonist's trust in an ally cracks after they witness them kill someone. Maybe the protagonist feels responsible for collateral damage. Violence should never be meaningless. It should always leave a mark.

The same goes for your antagonist. The best thriller villains aren't just violent—they're threatening. They understand how to use **implied violence** to control, manipulate, and terrify. Sometimes the most chilling villain isn't the one who pulls the trigger—it's the one who calmly promises they will.

You can ask ChatGPT to help you develop this kind of threat. Prompt, **"Write a scene where the antagonist threatens the protagonist without using physical violence."**

And here's something important: **Violence doesn't have to be physical.** Emotional violence, psychological threats, coercion, blackmail—all of these are weapons in a thriller. A villain revealing a protagonist's darkest secret in front of the world can be just as devastating as a bullet.

When you're writing your thriller in one day, it's easy to think you need to fill every chapter with action. But the truth is, well-placed, purposeful violence combined with constant threat is far more effective. It keeps the reader on edge without exhausting them.

Finally, remember that the **threat of violence can be more terrifying than the violence itself.** A loaded gun on the table. A villain's smile. A phone call with nothing but silence on the other end. That's what keeps readers turning pages long after midnight.

Writing a Compelling Opening Scene

There's no polite way to say this: in a thriller, if your opening scene doesn't hit hard, the reader's gone. You've lost them. There's no second chance. Thriller readers want to be grabbed by the throat from the very first line—and if you want to write a complete thriller in one day, you need to start strong and never let up. That means crafting an opening scene that's unputdownable, gripping, tense, and drenched in questions.

Your opening scene isn't just an introduction. It's a **promise**. You're promising your reader: this story will thrill you, twist you, shock you, and leave you breathless. So, how do you build that promise right from the first paragraph?

The key is understanding what an opening scene in a thriller needs to do. It has a job—and that job isn't to explain the backstory, describe the weather, or slowly ease the reader into the world. Its job is to **pull the reader into the story immediately and give them no reason to stop.**

Here's what a strong thriller opening scene should deliver:

1. Immediate Tension or Mystery.

Your story needs to open in the middle of something. A tense moment. A threat looming. A question unanswered. Readers don't care about setup—they care about what's happening right now. Open with a character in danger, a crime in progress, or a discovery that changes everything.

2. A Protagonist with Something at Stake.

The reader doesn't need to know the protagonist's full backstory yet, but they need to care about them. Show your protagonist facing a problem, a fear, or a choice that immediately puts them at risk—physically, emotionally, or morally.

3. A Hook That Raises Questions.

The best thriller openings plant a question in the reader's mind they can't ignore. What's really going on? Who's behind this? Why is the protagonist in danger? You want your reader to feel like they've been thrown into the middle of something dangerous and mysterious—and they need to keep reading to understand.

When you're writing fast, ChatGPT can help you generate these kinds of hooks instantly. Try prompting, **"Write an opening scene for a thriller that starts with immediate danger and a mysterious question."**

Let's look at a few ways you can structure an unputdownable opening:

Start with a Moment of Crisis.

Drop your protagonist into a scene where something's already gone wrong. A break-in. A chase. A murder. A betrayal. You don't have to explain everything yet—just show the chaos and let the reader figure it out alongside the protagonist.

Example:

He woke to the sound of glass shattering—and the cold edge of a knife at his throat.

Start with a Discovery.

Open with your protagonist finding something they shouldn't. A dead body. A hidden message. A piece of evidence that will unravel everything. The reader will immediately want to know what it means—and who doesn't want them to know it.

Example:

The envelope was waiting on her doorstep, no return address—just her name and a single word written beneath it: RUN.

Start with a Betrayal.

Open with a character being betrayed, lied to, or double-crossed. This immediately sets up emotional stakes and puts the reader on edge.

Example:

He shook the man's hand, smiled—and felt the cold weight of the pistol pressed against his spine.

When you're writing your thriller in one day, you can use ChatGPT to help you brainstorm and polish your opening. Try prompts like:

- **"Write a tense opening scene for a thriller where the protagonist is being followed."**
- **"How can I open this thriller story with immediate tension and a strong hook?"**

Another tip: **Start late, finish early.**

Don't waste time in your opening scene building up slowly to the action. Start when things are already happening. Cut the buildup. Throw the reader straight into the fire. And when the scene ends, leave them wanting more.

Show, don't tell.

In your opening, you don't need to explain everything. Let the reader experience the tension, the fear, the confusion alongside the protagonist. Use short, sharp sentences. Active verbs. Sensory details. Keep the focus tight.

Keep backstory to a minimum.

You can sprinkle in backstory and exposition later. The opening scene is not the place for it. Focus on the immediate moment and the immediate threat. Let the questions build.

Make it personal.

If you can, tie the opening scene directly to the protagonist's personal stakes. If they're being hunted, if their family's in danger, if they've just been betrayed—make it clear why this matters to them.

Here's an example of how you might structure a quick, punchy opening scene:

Paragraph one: Immediate sensory hook (gunshot, scream, crashing door). Paragraph two: Protagonist's reaction (fear, action, decision). Paragraph three: Introduce the immediate question or threat. Paragraph four: End on a cliffhanger.

You can use ChatGPT to help you draft and refine this quickly. Ask, **"Write a four-paragraph opening scene for a thriller that hooks the reader immediately and ends on a cliffhanger."**

Remember, your opening scene sets the tone. If you can hook the reader here, you can carry them through the entire story. And when you're writing a thriller in one day, a strong opening will give you the momentum you need to keep going.

Developing Twists Readers Never See Coming

Let's be real—when someone says, "That twist blew my mind," that's the gold medal for a thriller writer. Plot twists are what people remember. They're what get books recommended. They're what make a reader close the book, sit there in silence, and whisper, "No way." So, when you're writing your thriller in one day, you don't want twists that just surprise—you want twists that detonate.

But crafting a twist that readers never see coming **without cheating** is one of the toughest tricks in the thriller writer's playbook. The best twists don't just shock—they make sense. They reframe everything the reader thought they understood and, ideally, they've been hiding in plain sight the whole time.

So, how do you do it?

Let's start with the most important thing: **a twist isn't just a surprise.** A surprise is, "Boom! Here's something you didn't expect." A twist is, "Here's something you didn't expect, but now that you see it, everything clicks into place."

A good twist **changes the context** of everything that came before it. It adds a new lens to view earlier events. A character's lie. A missing detail. An emotional beat. That's why the best twists feel like punches and puzzles at the same time.

When you're planning your story, even quickly, build your twist from the **end backwards**. Start with what the twist is—maybe your trusted ally is the villain. Maybe the victim isn't really dead. Maybe your protagonist has been misled about the real goal the entire time. Whatever the twist is, work back through your story and look for **where to plant clues**.

This is where **foreshadowing** comes into play. You want to leave a breadcrumb trail, but make sure the crumbs are disguised. Use casual dialogue, throwaway details, or emotional beats that feel important for another reason. The reader should feel like you've been fair once the twist lands. They should say, "Wait—how did I miss that?" not, "That came out of nowhere."

You can use ChatGPT to help you plot this out. Prompt, **"What subtle clues can I include earlier in the story to foreshadow that [insert twist]?"**

A great technique is the **assumption reversal**. Most readers are constantly making assumptions as they read. That's good—it means they're engaged. Your job is to let them believe those assumptions and then flip them. If they assume a character is innocent, make them guilty. If they assume the villain is a stranger, make it someone close. If they think the protagonist knows what they're doing, reveal that they've been manipulated from the start.

To do this well, identify what your reader is most likely to assume at any given moment—and build your twist to knock that assumption down.

Another trick is **the misdirect**. You're not lying to the reader—you're just letting them look in the wrong direction. A classic misdirect involves making one character look suspicious while another quietly slips under the radar. You can even use a fake twist to distract from the real one. Lead the reader to believe they've figured it out, then pull the rug out from under them again.

Ask ChatGPT, **"How can I mislead the reader into suspecting the wrong character without making it too obvious?"**

When you reveal the twist, timing is everything. You want to hit it when the tension is high, the stakes are huge, and the protagonist thinks they've finally got things under control. That's when the twist should land like a hammer. Everything they thought they knew? Wrong. Everything they thought they'd solved? Just a piece of a bigger puzzle.

You can also drop a twist at the **midpoint** to shift the direction of the entire story. This is the "oh no" moment that takes the story deeper, darker, and more dangerous. Or you can save it for the **climax**, when it changes the final confrontation entirely.

And let's not forget the **emotional twist**. Not all great twists are about who the killer is or what the real plan was. Some of the best twists are internal. The character who's been fighting for justice realizes they're seeking revenge. The character who's been protecting someone discovers that person was never in danger—they were the threat. These kinds of twists cut deep because they're personal.

Twists work best when they tie into **character motivations**. If the twist is just about plot, it might surprise—but it won't hit as hard. If it reveals something about who your characters really are, that's when it sticks.

Let's look at an example:

Imagine your protagonist has been trying to expose a corporate conspiracy. They've been gathering evidence, staying one step ahead of a hired killer, and trusting one source—an insider who feeds them tips. But in the climax, they discover that the source was feeding them real information to **bury the bigger truth**—that the protagonist's own actions are being used as a smokescreen for something far worse. The source wasn't helping. They were **puppeteering**.

That twist doesn't just change the plot. It changes the protagonist's sense of purpose, their trust in their own instincts, and the moral weight of what they've done.

You can use ChatGPT to brainstorm this kind of twist fast. Try, **"Suggest a plot twist where the protagonist is being manipulated by someone they trust."** Or, **"Give me a twist that changes the reader's understanding of everything that came before."**

One final rule: **deliver, then move.** Once the twist hits, don't linger. Let the aftermath unfold, but don't over-explain. Trust the reader to feel the impact and ride the wave of new tension you've just created. Keep the momentum going.

In thrillers, a twist should never be the final word—it should be a door to even more chaos, conflict, or truth. So make it hit hard. Make it make sense. And make it matter.

Building Moral Ambiguity into Your Characters

If you want your thriller to feel grown-up, layered, and genuinely gripping—not just another popcorn page-turner—you need to learn how to play in the gray areas. That's where the most unforgettable thrillers live. Not in clean-cut heroes versus cartoon villains, but in that messy, uncomfortable space where everyone's motives are questionable, every decision has a price, and no one is entirely good or evil. That's the sweet spot of **moral ambiguity**.

When you're writing your thriller in one day, building morally ambiguous characters is one of the fastest ways to inject **depth, tension, and realism** into your story. Because when the reader can't quite figure out if they love or hate a character—or if the protagonist is even doing the right thing—that's when they stay hooked.

Let's get something straight first: moral ambiguity doesn't mean your characters are wishy-washy or inconsistent. It means they're human. They lie, cheat, betray, protect, justify, and make impossible choices—all while believing they're doing the right thing, or at least the only thing they can do.

So, how do you write characters like that?

Start with your **protagonist**. Forget the perfect hero. A thriller protagonist should be flawed. Maybe they've got a dark past. Maybe they're selfish, reckless, obsessive, or emotionally damaged. Maybe they're not entirely honest with themselves. They might even cross lines most people wouldn't—breaking the law, hurting others, making morally questionable deals—all in the name of a greater goal.

This doesn't make them unlikable. It makes them real. Readers will root for someone struggling with their own darkness, especially if they're fighting for something bigger than themselves.

You can use ChatGPT to help you shape this quickly. Prompt, **"What morally questionable traits could I give this thriller protagonist without making them unlikeable?"**

Next, look at your **antagonist**. The most chilling villains aren't the ones who are evil for evil's sake. They're the ones who believe they're right. Who think they're the hero of their own story. Who do terrible things for reasons the reader can almost understand.

If you want your antagonist to really stick with the reader, give them **sympathetic motives**. Maybe they're trying to protect someone they love. Maybe they're trying to fix a broken world. Maybe they're driven by revenge, and the reader can't help but think, **I might do the same in their shoes.**

You can ask ChatGPT, **"What sympathetic motive could I give this antagonist that clashes with the protagonist's goal?"**

Now, don't stop there. Your **supporting characters** should be morally gray, too. Allies who keep secrets. Mentors who betray. Friends who make selfish choices. In a thriller, trust is always fragile—and morally ambiguous side characters help keep that tension alive.

The key to writing these characters is to always ask: **What do they want? What are they willing to do to get it? And what line will they cross?**

When you're writing your thriller fast, you can use a simple exercise to build this in:

- For each major character, write down one thing they want.
- Write down one moral line they won't cross.
- Write down one moral line they will cross if pushed.

This helps you shape their gray areas quickly and keeps their actions consistent but complex.

Another important tool is **moral dilemmas**. Put your characters in situations where every choice is bad. Where doing the right thing costs too much. Where helping one person hurts another. This forces your characters to reveal who they really are—and keeps the reader on edge.

For example, your protagonist might have to choose between catching the villain or saving someone they love. They might have to work with a criminal to stop a worse threat. They might have to sacrifice their own freedom, reputation, or principles to do what's necessary.

These choices don't just drive the plot—they make the reader question what they would do in the same situation.

You can use ChatGPT to help you set these up. Ask, **"What moral dilemma could I put this protagonist in that would force them to compromise their values?"**

Another way to inject moral ambiguity is through **motivation versus action.** A character can have good motives but do terrible things. Or they can have selfish motives but end up doing the right thing anyway. This tension between why a character acts and what they actually do keeps readers guessing—and keeps the story layered.

For example, your protagonist might break the law to expose corruption. The antagonist might kill to protect their family. The ally might betray the protagonist to save themselves—but regret it later and try to make it right.

When you build this complexity into your characters, you also make your twists hit harder. If the reader believes a character is entirely good or bad, they'll see the twist coming. But if every character is morally ambiguous, every betrayal, reveal, or decision feels unpredictable and real.

One final thing: **don't judge your characters.** Let them make bad choices. Let them hurt people. Let them justify terrible things. Your job isn't to preach—it's to show the messiness of human nature and let the reader wrestle with it.

When you're writing your thriller in one day, you can use ChatGPT to help you add these layers quickly. Try prompts like:

- **"List five morally ambiguous traits for this protagonist."**
- **"Write a scene where the protagonist crosses a moral line to achieve their goal."**
- **"Describe how the antagonist justifies their actions."**

Thrillers live in the gray. The more you blur the lines between right and wrong, good and evil, hero and villain, the more gripping, memorable, and real your story will feel.

The Art of the Psychological Thriller

If there's one subgenre of thrillers that really messes with your head and stays under your skin long after you've finished the last page, it's the **psychological thriller**. These are the stories that don't just threaten the protagonist's life—they threaten their sanity, their beliefs, their grip on reality. And when you're writing a thriller in one day, weaving in psychological tension is one of the fastest ways to elevate your story from a simple chase to something deeper, darker, and far more compelling.

So, what makes a psychological thriller different?

At its core, a psychological thriller isn't about who will win the fight or whether the protagonist can outrun the antagonist. It's about **what's real and what's not**. It's about the mind games, manipulation, inner demons, and blurred lines between truth and lies. The real danger isn't just the villain—it's the protagonist's own mind.

When you understand this, you can start layering psychological tension into your story quickly and effectively.

The first thing you need is a **protagonist who's vulnerable**—not just physically, but mentally or emotionally. Maybe they're grieving, traumatized, or already on the edge when the story begins. Maybe they have a dark past, a secret addiction, or a fractured sense of self. The key is that their mind isn't a safe place. They can't trust what they see, hear, or even feel.

You can use ChatGPT to help you flesh this out quickly. Prompt, **"What internal fears or psychological vulnerabilities could I give this thriller protagonist?"**

Next, you need to create a story world that **feeds on uncertainty**. In a psychological thriller, the environment often reflects the protagonist's mental state. Settings can feel claustrophobic, surreal, or subtly wrong. Events can feel slightly off. The people around the protagonist might seem friendly—but something's missing, something's false.

The tension comes not just from external threats, but from the protagonist (and reader) questioning everything. Every ally could be an enemy. Every fact could be a lie. Every memory could be unreliable.

You can ask ChatGPT, **"Describe a setting that feels unsettling and psychologically tense without obvious danger."**

Another hallmark of the psychological thriller is the use of **unreliable narrators**. When your protagonist is cracking under pressure, lying to themselves, or hiding something even from the reader, it creates constant tension. Readers will keep turning pages, desperate to figure out what's real and what's not.

This doesn't mean your protagonist has to be insane. It means they have blind spots. They misinterpret things. They bury trauma. They can't see the full picture—and neither can the reader.

A classic way to do this is to use **internal monologue strategically**. Let the protagonist's thoughts spiral. Let their paranoia grow. Let them doubt everyone—including themselves. But keep the writing tight and tense so the reader feels that growing uncertainty.

You can use ChatGPT to help you sharpen this. Prompt, **"Write an internal monologue where the protagonist questions their own sanity in a tense moment."**

One of the best tricks of the psychological thriller is the **slow unraveling of truth**. You don't reveal everything up front. You let the reader—and the protagonist—peel back the layers, bit by bit, only to discover that everything they thought they knew was wrong.

This requires careful plotting, but it's something you can outline quickly when you're writing fast. Think about the big reveal you want at the end. Is the antagonist someone close to the protagonist? Is the protagonist's memory unreliable? Is the protagonist themselves the real threat?

Once you know the truth, you can plant **hints and misdirects** throughout your story without slowing down the pace. The goal is to make readers think they're figuring things out—only to pull the rug out from under them in the climax.

Ask ChatGPT, **"What subtle clues can I include in my psychological thriller to foreshadow the big reveal?"**

Themes are also crucial in a psychological thriller. These stories often deal with identity, memory, trauma, obsession, or the thin line between good and evil. You don't have to hit readers over the head with the theme, but letting it simmer under the surface gives your thriller more weight.

For example, if your theme is **trust**, you can structure your story so that every relationship in the protagonist's life is tested or shattered. If your theme is **guilt**, you can reveal that the protagonist is responsible for more than they realize.

You can use ChatGPT to brainstorm this quickly. Prompt, **"What theme could I explore in this psychological thriller, and how can I reflect it in the protagonist's journey?"**

The last piece of the puzzle is **atmosphere**. Psychological thrillers thrive on mood—dark, tense, suffocating. The language you use should reflect that. Short, sharp sentences. Sensory details that unsettle. Dialogue that's loaded with subtext and double meaning.

You can even experiment with perspective—switching between first-person and third-person, or using fragmented chapters to reflect the protagonist's fractured mental state. Don't be afraid to play with structure if it adds to the tension.

When you're writing your thriller in one day, you can quickly add this psychological layer by asking yourself:

- How can I make the protagonist question what's real?
- How can I make the reader doubt everything?
- What truth is hiding beneath the lies, and how can I reveal it slowly?

Psychological thrillers aren't about the body count. They're about the **mind games**. If you can make your reader doubt, question, and second-guess everything they're reading—all while racing to the end—you've nailed it.

Writing a Procedural Thriller with ChatGPT

Procedural thrillers are a special breed. They're the thrillers that suck you in with the details—the step-by-step investigation, the forensic clues, the meticulous unraveling of a crime. Think of shows like *CSI*, *Criminal Minds*, or movies like *Zodiac* and *Seven*. The action isn't always about shootouts or foot chases. It's about the process. The hunt. The methodical, sometimes obsessive search for the truth.

If you want to write a procedural thriller in one day, the good news is that ChatGPT can do a lot of the heavy lifting for you. You don't need to spend hours researching police protocols, forensics, or investigative procedures—you can have AI help you build a structured, believable, and thrilling investigation while you focus on the story's tension and emotional drive.

Let's break down how to do it.

First, understand what makes a procedural thriller tick. It's not just the crime—it's the **process of solving it.** Readers of procedural thrillers love following the trail, analyzing clues, connecting dots. They want to feel like they're inside the investigation, piecing it together alongside your protagonist. That means your thriller needs a strong, clear **case**. It could be a murder, a disappearance, a series of strange events that don't make sense. But it has to be something complex enough to require an investigation, with enough twists and layers to keep readers guessing.

When you're writing fast, start by asking ChatGPT to help you outline the case. Prompt, **"Create a complex crime plot suitable for a procedural thriller."** You'll instantly get ideas for crimes, victims, suspects, and possible motives.

Next, you need an **investigator protagonist**. This could be a detective, FBI agent, private investigator, journalist, or even an amateur sleuth with a reason to get involved. The key is that your protagonist is someone who's methodical, determined, and probably a little obsessive. You can use ChatGPT to help you flesh out their character quickly. Prompt, **"Create a morally complex detective protagonist for a procedural thriller."** Once you have your case and your protagonist, you need to structure the investigation itself. Procedural thrillers follow a clear rhythm:

- **A crime happens.**
- **The investigation begins.**
- **Clues and evidence are gathered.**
- **Suspects are identified and questioned.**
- **Red herrings and dead ends complicate the case.**
- **Breakthroughs lead to the real culprit.**
- **The climax delivers justice—or not.**

That structure gives you a solid spine for your story. You can use ChatGPT to outline the beats quickly. Prompt, **"Outline the major investigation steps in a procedural thriller about [insert case]."**

The tension in a procedural thriller doesn't come from explosions or chase scenes (although you can throw some in). It comes from the **unfolding puzzle**. Each new clue should raise more questions. Each suspect should have something to hide. Every time your protagonist thinks they're close to the truth, something should knock them back.

This is where you can use ChatGPT as a brainstorming partner. Ask, **"What obstacles or dead ends could complicate this investigation?"** or **"What misleading clues could I add to throw off the investigator?"**

One of the fastest ways to give your procedural thriller depth is to include **forensic and technical details**. Readers love the nitty-gritty—fingerprints, surveillance footage, autopsy reports, data analysis. You don't need to be an expert. You can use ChatGPT to generate these details quickly and accurately.

Try prompting, **"Describe the forensic evidence that could crack this case."** Or, **"What modern technology could help or hinder the investigation in this thriller?"**

But here's the thing: in a procedural thriller, the investigation is only half the story. The other half is **the investigator.** Their flaws, obsessions, relationships, and personal demons should bleed into the case. Maybe they're haunted by a similar crime. Maybe they're bending the rules. Maybe the case is forcing them to confront something they've buried.

This is what makes a procedural thriller gripping. The protagonist isn't just solving the crime—they're unraveling themselves.

When you're writing quickly, you can map this out easily. Ask yourself:

- What's the protagonist's personal stake in this case?
- What's their weakness or flaw?
- How does the case force them to confront it?

You can use ChatGPT to help you tie these threads together. Prompt, **"How can I connect the protagonist's personal struggles to the case in this procedural thriller?"**

Another hallmark of procedural thrillers is the **team dynamic**. Even if your protagonist is a lone wolf, they're going to interact with colleagues, superiors, forensic experts, or witnesses. These relationships create tension, conflict, and, sometimes, relief.

You don't need to create a massive cast when writing fast. But give your protagonist one or two supporting characters—an ally, a rival, a mentor—who challenge or help them.

Ask ChatGPT, **"Create a supporting cast of characters for this procedural thriller and describe their relationships with the protagonist."**

Finally, end your procedural thriller with a climax that's **earned**. No random confessions or last-minute evidence dumps. Readers want to see the protagonist put the pieces together, step by step, and solve the puzzle because they've done the work.

Whether the ending is triumphant, tragic, or morally ambiguous, it should feel like the logical, inevitable result of the investigation.

When you're writing your thriller in one day, procedural thrillers might seem intimidating because of the detail involved. But with the right structure and the help of ChatGPT, you can build a complex, layered story quickly—one that keeps readers glued to the page, racing to solve the case alongside your protagonist.

Global Stakes: Writing an International Thriller

If you want your thriller to feel big, dangerous, and epic—the kind of story that spans countries and cultures, that threatens the fate of nations or even the entire world—then you're writing an **international thriller**. These stories are packed with espionage, conspiracies, assassinations, global threats, and power players pulling strings behind closed doors. They move fast, jump borders, and always come with **high-stakes consequences.**

The best part is, when you're writing a thriller in one day, an international setting and global stakes instantly inject your story with scale and urgency without adding much extra effort. You don't need to write a James Bond franchise. You just need to know how to make the world feel wide and the stakes feel massive.

So, how do you pull this off without getting buried in research or overcomplicating the plot?

Let's start with the **stakes**. In an international thriller, the stakes aren't personal—they're global. We're talking terrorist attacks, political coups, the release of a deadly virus, nuclear threats, corporate espionage that could crash economies, or secret organizations manipulating world events. Your protagonist isn't just fighting to survive; they're fighting to stop something that will impact millions.

But here's the trick: while the stakes are global, the story still has to feel **personal**. Readers don't care about abstract threats. They care about people. So even if your protagonist is racing to stop a terrorist plot, the tension has to come from what's at stake **for them**. Maybe they've lost someone to a similar attack. Maybe they've been betrayed by their own government. Maybe the villain's goal will cost them everything.

You can use ChatGPT to help you map this out fast. Prompt, **"What global threat could drive the plot of an international thriller, and how can I tie it to the protagonist's personal stakes?"**

Once you've decided on the stakes, it's time to build your **global setting**. International thrillers move. They hop from city to city, continent to continent. Paris, London, Moscow, Dubai, Tokyo, New York—the world is your playground.

But don't let this intimidate you. You don't need to write a travel guide. You just need to choose a handful of locations that serve the story and give the reader a sense of scope.

Pick locations that:

- **Reflect the tension.** A back alley in Istanbul. A train station in Berlin. A political summit in Washington.
- **Provide obstacles.** Language barriers, cultural differences, unfamiliar environments.
- **Add flavor and atmosphere.** Give the reader a taste of these places without slowing down the action.

You can use ChatGPT to speed this up. Prompt, **"List five international locations that could create tension and danger in a thriller."** Then, when writing, use sharp, sensory details—a smell, a sound, a piece of architecture—to ground the scene quickly.

Next, let's talk about **antagonists**. In an international thriller, your villain is usually powerful, connected, and ruthless. They're not just some local thug. They're a politician, a corporate mogul, a terrorist leader, or a shadowy figure pulling strings behind the scenes. They have global reach, and they're willing to do whatever it takes to get what they want.

But again, keep it personal. Give your villain a motive that makes sense—money, power, revenge, ideology. The more human and complex they are, the more dangerous they'll feel.

You can use ChatGPT to help you craft this. Prompt, **"Create a morally complex villain for an international thriller with global ambitions."**

Now, structure is key. International thrillers move fast, and they're usually built like a **race against time**. The protagonist uncovers a piece of the puzzle in one country, then has to move to the next location to follow the next lead. Each scene should escalate the tension, with new obstacles, betrayals, and revelations pushing the protagonist closer to the edge.

Think of it like a chain reaction. Each clue, each encounter, each betrayal leads to the next location, the next conflict, the next cliffhanger.

When writing quickly, you can map this out fast with ChatGPT. Ask, **"Outline the locations and key events of a fast-paced international thriller."**

One of the best things about international thrillers is the opportunity to include **espionage, politics, and power games**. Double agents, secret alliances, political corruption, private military contractors—you can throw all of these into the mix to keep the reader guessing.

But don't overload your plot. Pick two or three key conspiracies or power players and focus on how they intersect with the protagonist's mission.

Moral ambiguity also thrives in international thrillers. Governments covering up crimes. Intelligence agencies sacrificing innocent lives. The protagonist being forced to work with bad people to stop something worse. The lines between good and evil blur at the international level, and that's where your story's tension can explode.

You can ask ChatGPT, **"Suggest ways to weave political and moral ambiguity into an international thriller plot."**

And don't forget: an international thriller is still a **thriller**. That means you need to keep the pacing tight. Use short chapters, cliffhanger endings, escalating stakes, and constant forward momentum. Even when your characters are sitting in a briefing room or decoding a message, the tension should be there.

In your climax, bring it all home. The puzzle pieces should click together. The protagonist should face their personal and external stakes in one final, nail-biting confrontation. And the global threat should come down to a single, clear moment—defuse the bomb, expose the conspiracy, stop the assassination.

When you're writing a thriller in one day, the international thriller is one of the easiest ways to make your story feel **big, dangerous, and unstoppable**. You can use real-world locations, current events, and political tensions to fuel your plot, and ChatGPT can help you fill in the details quickly so you can focus on the tension, twists, and characters.

How to Blend Crime, Mystery, and Thriller Together

If you've been reading thrillers for any length of time, you'll know something interesting: the lines between **crime**, **mystery**, and **thriller** blur all the time. Some of the best stories out there don't stick to one box. They steal elements from all three and mix them into something fast, addictive, and impossible to put down. And when you're writing a thriller in one day, learning how to blend these genres is one of the quickest ways to give your story depth, tension, and layers without slowing you down.

So, how do you do it?

First, you need to understand the difference between these three genres.

Crime fiction is about the crime itself. There's usually a murder, a heist, or some other criminal act at the center of the story. The tension often comes from who committed the crime, why, and whether justice will be served.

Mystery fiction is about solving the puzzle. The crime has already happened, and the story follows the detective, investigator, or amateur sleuth as they put the pieces together.

Thrillers are about danger, tension, and urgency. The crime or mystery is often unfolding in real time, and the protagonist isn't just trying to solve something—they're trying to survive.

When you blend all three, you get a story that's smart, fast, dangerous, and layered—a story where the reader is trying to solve the puzzle, feel the threat, and understand the crime all at once.

The easiest way to start blending is to build your story around a **crime with high stakes and a mystery at its core**. Think about a murder, disappearance, heist, or conspiracy that's not only dangerous but also puzzling. Something that isn't just about catching the bad guy—but about understanding what's really going on.

For example, instead of writing a straightforward murder mystery, you can have the murder trigger a larger conspiracy. The protagonist isn't just solving who killed someone—they're uncovering a web of lies and danger that puts them at risk.

You can use ChatGPT to help you map this out fast. Prompt, **"Create a plot for a thriller that blends crime, mystery, and high-stakes danger."**

Next, focus on **pacing and structure.**

The mystery element gives your story a puzzle to solve. The crime element provides the stakes. The thriller element gives it speed and danger. Your structure should reflect that:

Start with a **crime**—something shocking, violent, or mysterious enough to hook the reader.

Layer in the **mystery**—who did it, why, how? Let the protagonist and reader uncover clues, face dead ends, and question everything.

Fuel it all with **thriller pacing**—short chapters, constant danger, cliffhangers, twists, betrayals, and a clear sense that if the protagonist doesn't solve this, it will cost them everything.

One thing to keep in mind is how you reveal information. In a mystery, the tension comes from what the protagonist doesn't know. In a thriller, the tension comes from what the protagonist does know—and what they do about it. When blending the two, you can play with both.

For example, your protagonist might discover the murderer halfway through—but that's when the thriller kicks in, because now they have to stop something worse from happening.

You can use ChatGPT to help you plan these reveals. Prompt, **"Outline how to reveal key pieces of the mystery gradually while escalating the thriller tension."**

Another powerful tool is to use **multiple points of view**. In a mystery, you often stick to the investigator's perspective. In a thriller, you might jump between the protagonist and the antagonist. In crime fiction, you might include the criminal's perspective.

When you blend the three, you can use shifting perspectives strategically:

- Let the reader see the crime from the criminal's point of view.
- Let them follow the investigator's growing obsession.
- Let them experience the protagonist's fear and danger.

This keeps the reader guessing and makes the tension feel alive.

You can ask ChatGPT, **"Create a chapter outline for a crime-mystery-thriller with multiple perspectives."**

Another thing to keep in mind is **theme**. The best blended thrillers aren't just about what happens—they're about something bigger. Corruption. Justice. Revenge. Identity. Morality. The more layers you add, the more compelling your story becomes.

For example, your protagonist might be hunting a killer (crime), uncovering a hidden conspiracy (mystery), and racing against time to prevent another attack (thriller)—but the real story is about how far they're willing to go to get the truth, and what it will cost them.

You can ask ChatGPT to help you tie this together. Prompt, **"What central theme could I explore in a thriller that blends crime and mystery?"**

One more tip: don't forget the **emotional stakes**. Crime, mystery, and thriller elements give your story structure and plot—but emotion gives it heart. Make sure your protagonist has something personal to lose. A loved one in danger. A past mistake they're trying to fix. A moral line they don't want to cross but might have to.

When you blend genres, the danger is that the story becomes too intellectual—just a puzzle to solve. You need the emotional engine to keep the reader invested.

The beauty of writing a blended thriller in one day is that you can lean on structure. Your crime gives you an inciting incident. Your mystery gives you a puzzle. Your thriller pacing keeps the reader hooked. And with ChatGPT helping you map out clues, twists, and tension points, you can build a layered, gripping story fast.

Injecting Real-World Fears into Your Story

One of the secret weapons of a truly gripping thriller isn't found in clever plot twists or car chases—it's found in tapping into the fears your reader already carries with them. The most memorable thrillers feel real because they lean into **real-world fears**. And when you're writing a thriller in one day, injecting these fears into your story is one of the fastest ways to give it depth, weight, and urgency.

So, what exactly are real-world fears?

They're the anxieties, dangers, and what-if scenarios that keep people awake at night. They're rooted in reality, or at least in the possibility of reality. They're things people are already worried about—government surveillance, corporate corruption, terrorism, pandemics, political conspiracies, financial collapse, nuclear war, cybercrime, kidnapping, human trafficking, betrayal, psychological breakdown. The things people read in the news and quietly think, **What if that happened to me?**

When you tap into those fears, you don't just entertain your reader—you pull them into the story emotionally and psychologically. You make them uncomfortable in the best possible way.

The first step is to decide **which real-world fear you want to play with**. You don't need to jam in every possible threat. Pick one core fear that will drive your thriller.

You can use ChatGPT to help you brainstorm quickly. Prompt, **"List real-world fears I can use to build tension in a thriller story."**

For example, maybe your story revolves around:

- **A corporate conspiracy** where a pharmaceutical giant is suppressing a cure for profit.
- **A political thriller** where the protagonist uncovers a plot to rig an election.
- **A tech thriller** where someone's digital identity is hacked and used against them.
- **A psychological thriller** where the protagonist fears they're losing their mind.

Once you know the core fear, you can start weaving it into every layer of your story.

One way to do this is to use the **setting and atmosphere** to reflect the fear. If your story is about surveillance, make your settings cold, impersonal, full of cameras and technology. If it's about corporate corruption, set your scenes in gleaming skyscrapers that feel hollow and dangerous. If it's about psychological breakdown, create claustrophobic, disorienting environments.

You can use ChatGPT to help build this quickly. Prompt, **"Describe a setting that reflects the fear of [insert real-world fear]."**

Next, filter that fear through your **characters**. Your protagonist should embody the fear in some way. Maybe they're paranoid about being watched. Maybe they're terrified of losing control. Maybe they've been burned by the system before and are driven by that trauma.

But don't stop with the protagonist. Let your antagonist exploit that fear. Let your supporting characters reflect different ways people deal with it—denial, obsession, resignation, rebellion.

You can ask ChatGPT, **"How can I tie the fear of [insert real-world fear] into the protagonist's personal stakes?"**

Another powerful tool is to use **small, relatable details** to ground the fear. Readers connect most when the threat feels like it could happen to them. Show how your protagonist's phone is being tracked. Show them watching a news report about something similar to the threat they're facing. Show them worrying about their family, their freedom, their safety.

These little moments pull the fear out of the abstract and into the reader's living room.

And here's the thing: you don't have to make the fear the entire plot. It can just be the **background radiation** that colors the story. Maybe the protagonist is solving a personal mystery—but it's happening against the backdrop of political unrest or rising cybercrime.

When writing fast, ChatGPT can help you layer this in without slowing down. Ask, **"What background events could reflect the fear of [insert real-world fear] in a thriller setting?"**

Another reason to lean into real-world fears is that it gives your thriller **relevance**. Readers love thrillers that feel timely, ripped from the headlines, or eerily possible. It makes the tension hit harder because it feels like it could happen tomorrow.

You can even play with **reader expectations**. If your thriller is about government surveillance, your reader might expect the villain to be a government agent. Twist that expectation. Make it someone close to the protagonist, using the system against them. Make the threat feel more personal.

One word of caution: Don't turn your thriller into a political lecture or social commentary essay. The real-world fear should be part of the story's tension—not the story itself. Readers want to be entertained, not preached at.

Instead, let the fear shape the plot, characters, and atmosphere. Let it color every decision, every obstacle, every twist.

Here's an example:

Let's say your thriller is about bio-terrorism. The fear of a global pandemic is the real-world fear. Your protagonist is a scientist trying to stop an outbreak. Along the way, you can layer in:

- News reports of rising infections.
- Government cover-ups.
- Public panic and misinformation.
- The protagonist's own fear of losing someone they love.

You can use ChatGPT to help you map this out. Prompt, **"Outline how to incorporate the fear of bio-terrorism into every act of a thriller story."**

The best part is, when you build your thriller around a real-world fear, you don't have to work as hard to create tension. The fear is already baked into the reader's mind. You're just tapping into it, reminding them of what's possible, and then turning the dial to eleven.

Researching for Authenticity without Getting Stuck

One of the easiest traps thriller writers fall into—especially when writing something as layered and complex as a crime, mystery, or international thriller—is the **black hole of research.** You start by looking up how fingerprint analysis works and two hours later, you're reading about 1980s CIA operations in South America. It's easy to lose entire days researching, convincing yourself you "need to know everything" before you can start writing.

But here's the thing: **you don't.**

When you're writing a thriller in one day, research can't be a rabbit hole. It has to be a tool—something you use quickly and efficiently to give your story authenticity without slowing you down or stealing your creative momentum.

The goal isn't to become an expert in police procedure, cyber warfare, or international politics. The goal is to know **just enough** to make the story feel real. Readers want the sense that the world you've created could exist—they don't need a textbook.

So, how do you research fast and smart without getting stuck?

Start with the **basics.** Before you write, figure out what specific knowledge you actually need. Don't research everything. Research only what's **story-critical.** Ask yourself:

- What is the crime, threat, or central mystery in my thriller?
- What procedural, technical, or factual details do I need to make that believable?
- What locations, organizations, or technologies appear in my story?

Once you've got that list, focus your research like a laser beam. You don't need to know how every department of the FBI operates—you just need to know how an agent would get jurisdiction in your story's context. You don't need to understand how every type of bomb is built—you need to know how one bomb works, the one in your plot.

When you're writing fast, use ChatGPT to help you shortcut research. For example, prompt:

- **"Summarize how an FBI investigation works in a murder case."**
- **"Describe how a black-market arms deal would be set up."**
- **"Give me quick facts about surveillance technology used by intelligence agencies."**

This will give you enough info to add realism without slowing down.

Another great way to keep your research under control is to use the **"good enough" rule.** You're writing fiction, not a technical manual. Your job is to **sound like you know what you're talking about** without overwhelming the reader with jargon. Most readers aren't experts—they won't notice if you fudge a detail or simplify a process as long as it feels real.

For instance, if you're writing about a forensic lab, you don't need to know every chemical used to lift fingerprints. You need to know that fingerprints are dusted, analyzed, and matched through a database—and how to describe that process in a few punchy lines.

If you do get stuck on something specific, ask ChatGPT for a **story-friendly explanation.** Prompt, **"Explain how DNA evidence is collected and matched in a way that makes sense for a thriller scene."**

Dialogue and character behavior are another area where authenticity matters. If you're writing a procedural thriller, you want your cops, detectives, or agents to sound like they know what they're doing. But you don't need to reproduce real-life conversations word for word—you just need to capture the tone.

Use research to sprinkle in **authentic language and procedure** without bogging down your dialogue. Ask ChatGPT, **"What slang or shorthand would a homicide detective use at a crime scene?"** That's enough to sell the realism without writing a training manual.

Locations are another research trap. International thrillers, especially, tempt writers to spend hours researching city streets, customs, or local politics. But readers don't need a travel guide—they need atmosphere and tension. Instead of memorizing every landmark in Berlin or Tokyo, focus on **three to five sensory details** that make the scene come alive: the smell of street food, the sound of sirens, the cold stone of an alleyway.

You can ask ChatGPT, **"Give me five atmospheric details to describe a chase scene in Rome."** Boom—you're ready to write.

The same rule applies to weapons, vehicles, technology, and anything else technical. Readers want authenticity—but they want it delivered quickly, through the lens of tension and story. Don't get stuck researching every model of handgun or every function of an encrypted phone. Find one or two believable details and move on.

A great trick when writing fast is to **leave placeholders.** If you don't know something in the moment—how long it would take to get from Paris to Zurich, what protocol an Interpol agent would follow—don't stop writing to research. Just drop a placeholder like [**INSERT RESEARCH HERE**] and keep going. You can fill in the gaps later.

Another way to avoid getting stuck is to **limit yourself to research sessions.** Set a timer for 10 or 15 minutes. Research what you need, gather enough facts to make your scene believable, and then close the tabs and keep writing. You can always clean up later.

And here's the real secret: **Most of the authenticity comes from how your characters react, not from the technical details.** If your protagonist is a detective, make them act like one—methodical, observant, driven. If they're a spy, make them suspicious, precise, morally compromised. Readers will buy the world you're creating because the people in it feel real, not because you accurately described how a wiretap works.

When you're writing your thriller in one day, research is a tool, not a barrier. Use it strategically. Stay focused. Use AI to speed up the process. And remember: the goal isn't to impress experts—it's to keep your reader hooked, breathless, and turning pages.

Writing from the Villain's Perspective

If you really want to give your thriller teeth—if you want to make it pulse, crackle, and get under your reader's skin—then you need to do one thing that most beginner thriller writers avoid: **get inside the villain's head**.

The best thrillers aren't just about a clever protagonist. They're about a terrifying, cunning, or emotionally complex villain who feels so real that readers can't help but be fascinated. And one of the fastest, most effective ways to bring that villain to life—especially when you're writing a thriller in one day—is to write parts of your story from **their perspective**.

It doesn't have to be half the book. Even just a handful of scenes, chapters, or glimpses into the villain's point of view can inject your story with an edge of danger that never lets up.

So, why does writing from the villain's perspective work so well?

Because it gives your story **dramatic irony and tension.**

The reader knows something the protagonist doesn't. They know what the villain is planning, what they want, how far they'll go. That knowledge creates a ticking clock effect—the reader's on edge, waiting to see how long it will take for the protagonist to catch up, or whether they'll survive when they finally collide.

When you write these villain scenes, the first thing to remember is this: **Your villain doesn't think they're the villain.** They believe they're right. They believe they're justified. Maybe they believe the world is broken, and they're the only one brave enough to fix it. Maybe they think they're protecting someone, avenging a wrong, or balancing the scales.

The more human your villain is, the scarier they become. Because the reader will see themselves in them—and that's unsettling.

You can use ChatGPT to help you flesh this out quickly. Prompt, **"Create a morally complex villain who believes they're the hero of their own story."**

Another reason to write from the villain's perspective is that it lets you show **the scope of the threat.** From the protagonist's point of view, the villain is a shadowy figure pulling strings in the background. But from the villain's point of view, you can reveal the full scope of their resources, connections, ruthlessness, and reach. You can show them plotting, manipulating, eliminating obstacles.

This is especially powerful in an international thriller, crime thriller, or psychological thriller, where the villain's moves shape the world the protagonist is stumbling through.

When you're writing fast, you can structure these villain POV scenes like brief, sharp interludes.

Drop them in between your protagonist's chapters like a ticking clock. Each time the reader sees the villain, they should:

1. **Learn something terrifying.**
2. **See the villain's emotional or psychological depth.**
3. **Feel the countdown accelerating.**

You can ask ChatGPT, **"Write a short, tense scene from the villain's perspective that reveals their next move without spoiling the twist."**

Another benefit of writing villain POV scenes is that they give you a place to build **theme and atmosphere** without slowing down your protagonist's storyline. The villain's perspective can explore the story's darker themes—power, revenge, control, obsession—and deepen the reader's understanding of what's at stake.

But here's the key: Don't overexplain.

You don't want to reveal every detail of the villain's plan. You want to show their mindset, their process, their drive—but keep enough back so that the protagonist (and the reader) still has questions. You want the reader to know how dangerous the villain is without giving away how everything will unfold.

Think of these villain chapters like little puzzle pieces. Each one shows more of the picture—but the full image only clicks into place at the climax.

One powerful trick is to write these villain scenes in a **cold, clinical, or detached tone**. Contrast the protagonist's emotional, frantic, personal perspective with the villain's cool, methodical mindset. It creates a rhythm in your story—one side racing to survive, the other calmly planning destruction.

Or flip it. Make the villain **chaotic, unstable, emotionally charged.** Let the reader see how unhinged they are, how close they are to snapping, how dangerous their unpredictability makes them.

You can use ChatGPT to help you nail the voice quickly. Prompt, **"Write a tense scene in the villain's voice, showing their calm detachment as they plan something terrible."** Or, **"Write a chaotic, unstable monologue from a villain losing control."**

Another tool is to use villain POV scenes to **foreshadow your twists.** Let the villain mention something cryptic. Let them reveal a relationship to another character that the protagonist doesn't know about yet. Let them hint at their real goal in a way that only makes sense when the final twist lands.

A few well-placed villain chapters can also keep your middle act tight and tense. When you feel the story slowing down, drop in a villain scene to crank the tension back up.

And finally, make sure you deliver **emotional payoff**. Readers don't want a cartoon villain twirling their mustache. They want a villain who feels like a real, breathing person with a purpose, a philosophy, and real pain or passion driving them.

That's what makes the final confrontation satisfying—not just that the villain is defeated, but that their defeat means something. That the reader understands how close they came to winning—and how much the protagonist had to sacrifice to stop them.

When you're writing your thriller in one day, villain POV scenes are one of the fastest ways to add tension, complexity, and depth without slowing the story down. You don't need a full backstory or long monologues—just sharp, tense snapshots that show the reader the enemy's face.

Exploring the Theme of Trust in a Thriller

If you peel back the layers of almost any thriller—whether it's a hard-hitting procedural, a psychological mind-bender, or an international race against time—you'll almost always find one central theme lurking beneath all the tension: **trust.** Who can be trusted? Who's lying? Who's hiding something? Can the protagonist even trust themselves?

Thrillers live and breathe in that space where trust is fragile, shifting, and dangerously unreliable. And when you're writing a thriller in one day, anchoring your story around the theme of trust is one of the fastest ways to give it emotional weight, narrative tension, and thematic depth without overcomplicating the plot.

So how do you do it?

The first step is to recognize that trust isn't just a theme—it's a **weapon** in a thriller. Trust is built, broken, and manipulated throughout the story. Every character's choices, every betrayal, every twist feeds into it. The more you mess with trust, the more tense your story becomes.

Start with your **protagonist.**

Your protagonist's journey in a thriller is almost always about navigating a minefield of lies, secrets, and shifting loyalties. Maybe they start the story trusting too easily—and it gets them hurt. Maybe they trust no one—and that paranoia isolates them and makes things worse. Maybe they've been betrayed before and are struggling to trust again.

When writing fast, you can use ChatGPT to help you define this quickly. Prompt, **"What trust issues could this thriller protagonist have, and how could they shape the story?"**

You also want to tie the theme of trust to your **protagonist's arc.**

How does their relationship with trust change from the start of the story to the end? Maybe they start off cynical and unwilling to rely on anyone, but by the climax, they have to trust an unlikely ally to survive. Or maybe they start out believing in a person or institution—and by the end, they realize that trust was misplaced and dangerous.

That emotional shift gives your thriller weight beyond the action.

Now, let's talk about your **supporting cast.**

In a thriller, every supporting character is a potential threat. Even the protagonist's closest allies should carry the risk of betrayal. The reader should constantly be asking: **Can this person be trusted?**

You can use trust as a tension device in dialogue, action, and behavior. Maybe a partner seems too eager to help. Maybe a family member hides something. Maybe a friend has a secret past connection to the antagonist.

When you're writing your thriller quickly, use ChatGPT to brainstorm. Prompt, **"List ways supporting characters in this thriller can appear trustworthy but later reveal they're hiding something."**

One of the most effective ways to explore trust in your thriller is to use **misdirection and betrayal.**

Set up a character the reader trusts—then pull the rug out. Make an ally a double agent. Make a victim a villain. Or go deeper: show a character who betrays the protagonist not because they're evil, but because they've been forced into an impossible choice.

These betrayals don't just create great plot twists—they challenge the reader emotionally. They force the protagonist (and the audience) to question everything.

But trust isn't just about who betrays whom. It's also about **how people rebuild trust after it's broken.**

A powerful moment in any thriller is when two characters, battered by lies and violence, finally drop their guard and trust each other. Maybe it's in the middle of a firefight. Maybe it's during a tense conversation where everything hangs in the balance. That moment of human connection makes the danger hit harder.

You can ask ChatGPT, **"Write a tense scene where two thriller characters finally decide to trust each other after a betrayal."**

Another place where trust plays a crucial role is in the thriller's **psychological tension.**

In a psychological thriller, trust often breaks down internally. The protagonist doesn't just question the people around them—they question their own memories, instincts, and sanity. The enemy isn't just outside—it's inside their own head.

This kind of internal conflict adds another layer to the theme. The protagonist's struggle to trust themselves becomes the emotional engine of the story.

You can also use trust to shape your **plot structure.**

Design your story so that each act is shaped by trust:

- In Act One, the protagonist trusts the wrong people.
- In Act Two, that trust is shattered.
- In Act Three, they must decide who (if anyone) they can trust to survive.

And in the climax, make the protagonist face one final test of trust. Maybe they have to put their life in the hands of someone who betrayed them. Maybe they have to risk everything on a fragile alliance. Maybe they have to trust themselves to make the right choice when the stakes couldn't be higher.

One of the best tools for writing this quickly is to use ChatGPT to map out those trust shifts. Prompt, **"Outline how the protagonist's trust in key characters changes across each act of this thriller."**

Finally, don't forget that the theme of trust doesn't have to be stated outright. You don't need characters delivering long speeches about trust and betrayal. Instead, let it live in the actions, decisions, and consequences. Let the reader feel it in every risk, every lie, every moment when the protagonist doesn't know who to believe.

Trust is the engine that drives tension in a thriller. The more fragile, complex, and dangerous trust becomes in your story, the more your readers will be glued to the page.

How to Balance Action with Character Development

One of the biggest challenges thriller writers face—especially when trying to write an entire thriller in one day—is finding the sweet spot between heart-pounding **action** and meaningful **character development**. It's easy to think you need to sacrifice one for the other, that you can either have constant car chases, fights, and narrow escapes, or you can slow everything down and dive into your characters' emotions and backstory.

But the truth is, the best thrillers do both at the same time. And if you can learn how to balance action with character development, your story will hit harder, feel more real, and keep your reader glued to the page all the way to the final twist.

So, how do you do it?

First, let's talk about why this balance matters.

Action without character development is like watching someone else play a video game. Sure, the explosions and shootouts are cool—but if you don't care about the person holding the controller, you'll check out fast. On the flip side, character development without action can kill the pace of a thriller. If your characters spend entire chapters sitting around thinking about their childhood trauma while the world is burning outside, your reader will get bored.

You want the reader to care about your protagonist's internal struggles **because those struggles are woven into the external action.**

One of the fastest and easiest ways to balance this when writing quickly is to make sure every action scene is also a **character scene.**

That means every fight, chase, or confrontation should reveal something about your protagonist:

- Their skills
- Their fears
- Their moral lines
- Their past mistakes
- Their relationships

For example, if your protagonist is in a fistfight, don't just describe the punches. Show how they hesitate when they realize the person they're fighting knows something about their past. Or how they snap and go too far because they're haunted by something they can't forgive themselves for.

You can use ChatGPT to help with this. Prompt, **"Write an action scene where the protagonist's internal struggle is revealed through their choices during the fight."**

Another trick is to use **reaction beats** immediately after action scenes. Once the dust settles, give your protagonist a moment—just a few lines—to reflect, struggle, or connect with another character. You don't need long monologues or flashbacks. Just a brief, sharp emotional beat that shows how the action has changed them or what it cost them.

This could be as simple as the protagonist realizing they almost killed someone and questioning who they're becoming. Or recognizing that their ally risked everything to save them—and feeling the weight of that loyalty.

When writing your thriller fast, you can even plan this in your outline. For every big action scene, make a note: **What does this reveal about the protagonist? What choice or regret follows this?**

You can ask ChatGPT, **"Suggest an emotional aftermath scene for this action sequence in my thriller."**

Dialogue during action scenes is another tool for developing character without slowing the pace. Let your protagonist and supporting characters argue, reveal secrets, or show vulnerability even while they're under fire. Tense conversations while driving too fast, fighting for their lives, or running from danger can reveal personality, relationships, and backstory.

It's also a great place to inject humor, humanity, or tension-breaking moments. Readers love seeing who your characters are when they're under pressure.

Another strategy is to let your protagonist's **internal conflicts fuel the action.**

If your protagonist has unresolved guilt, let it drive them to take reckless risks. If they're struggling to trust someone, make that tension explode during a high-stakes operation. If they're trying to prove themselves, show how far they're willing to go—and how that almost destroys them.

This is what makes action scenes mean something. They're not just spectacle. They're a window into who your characters are.

And don't forget your **antagonist.**

Your villain's actions should also reveal their character. Their choices in tense situations should show their ruthlessness, cunning, or even their humanity. When your villain makes a move, it should reflect their values, fears, or weaknesses—not just advance the plot.

You can use ChatGPT to help you tighten this up. Prompt, **"Write a scene where the villain's actions reveal their internal conflict during an intense moment."**

A common mistake is to try and separate the action and character development into different parts of the story—action in the first half, character reflection in the second, or vice versa. But the most effective thrillers **blend them scene by scene.**

The action should shape the characters. The characters' choices should shape the action. Each should fuel the other.

When you're writing fast, you can keep this balance simple:

- In every action scene, ask: **What does this reveal about the characters?**
- In every quiet scene, ask: **How does this build tension for the next action moment?**

That constant back-and-forth creates momentum. Your story never feels like it's pausing for a character study, but your reader is still learning, feeling, and connecting with your protagonist.

And here's a final tip: **use pacing to your advantage.**

Short, sharp action scenes. Quick emotional beats. Let the adrenaline and the character development dance together in a rhythm that keeps the reader hooked.

When you master this balance—when your action isn't just spectacle, but character-driven—you'll have a thriller that readers can't put down. Because they won't just want to know what happens next. They'll want to know **who your protagonist becomes** by the end of the fight.

In the next chapter, we'll look at how to use **the ticking clock technique** to crank up the tension and keep your reader racing toward the climax.

The Power of Deadlines, Time Limits, and Ticking Clocks

If there's one storytelling trick guaranteed to crank up the tension and glue your reader to the page, it's the simple but devastating power of the **ticking clock**. Nothing drives urgency, stakes, and suspense quite like a clear deadline. Whether it's a literal clock counting down to an explosion or an emotional deadline that's closing in, a time limit is one of the fastest and most effective ways to inject energy into your thriller.

And when you're writing a thriller in one day, it's one of the easiest structural tools you can build into your story to make sure it never sags.

So, why do ticking clocks work so well?

Because they make every scene matter.

They give your protagonist—and your reader—a constant sense of pressure. There's no room to breathe, no time to hesitate. Every decision, every mistake, every delay has consequences.

The beauty of the ticking clock is that it's incredibly flexible. It can be:

- A literal countdown: A bomb set to detonate in 12 hours.
- A personal deadline: A ransom demand with a time limit.
- A situational constraint: The protagonist has 48 hours before a witness disappears.
- A psychological time limit: The protagonist's mental state is deteriorating fast.
- A procedural deadline: An investigation has to be solved before a political event.
- An existential threat: The world will end in seven days if the protagonist fails.

You can use ChatGPT to help you brainstorm quickly. Prompt, **"List creative ticking clock scenarios for a thriller story."**

When you're writing your thriller fast, building a deadline into your plot helps you structure your story naturally. It gives you a clear framework:

- **Act One:** Introduce the time limit and the stakes.
- **Act Two:** Show how the clock keeps ticking down, with obstacles, false leads, and escalating tension.
- **Act Three:** Bring the protagonist to the final seconds of the deadline, forcing them into an impossible choice.

That clock is like a drumbeat under your story. Even when there's no action scene happening, the reader feels the pressure.

A good ticking clock also shapes your characters.

Deadlines force people to show who they really are. Some rise to the challenge. Some crumble. Some cut corners. Some make dangerous alliances. When the clock is ticking, your characters can't afford to play it safe—and neither can your reader.

You can even use the clock to expose your protagonist's flaws. Maybe they've wasted time in the past and now they're paying for it. Maybe they make a rash decision because they're running out of time. Maybe they push someone away because they're so focused on the deadline that they lose sight of what's important.

Another trick is to use the ticking clock to **mislead your reader.**

You can set up a visible deadline—say, 24 hours to stop a bomb—but then reveal halfway through that the real deadline is sooner, or that the clock itself is a distraction and the real threat is something else.

You can use ChatGPT to help you map this out. Prompt, **"Outline a thriller plot where the protagonist thinks they have more time than they actually do."**

One of the best ways to make the clock work is to **keep reminding the reader.**

Drop time checks into your scene transitions. Let characters mention how much time is left. Show the clock ticking down in the background of action scenes. Make the reader feel like they're racing alongside the protagonist.

For example:

"Five hours left. And he was no closer to finding the last piece of the puzzle."

Or:

"She glanced at her watch again. Forty-three minutes. It wasn't enough."

These little reminders keep the tension alive even when nothing explosive is happening.

You can also use the deadline to shape your **story's pacing.**

In the first act, the clock is introduced, but there's breathing room. The protagonist has time to gather clues, make plans, figure things out.

In the second act, the clock tightens. Every minute lost is another nail in the coffin. Obstacles multiply. Mistakes cost more.

In the third act, the clock is almost gone. Everything happens fast. Decisions are made in the heat of the moment. There's no room to pause, no safety net.

That pacing rhythm keeps your story moving forward and gives your reader no choice but to keep turning pages.

And here's the best part:

A ticking clock doesn't have to end with the clock running out. You can pull off a last-second save. You can let the protagonist fail spectacularly. You can twist the ending so that the deadline wasn't what everyone thought it was. But the pressure of that clock will shape everything leading up to the climax.

When you're writing a thriller in one day, building your plot around a deadline is like giving yourself a roadmap. It keeps your pacing tight, your stakes high, and your characters under constant, relentless pressure.

You can use ChatGPT to help you refine this fast. Prompt, **"Create a thriller outline where a ticking clock forces the protagonist into escalating decisions."**

How to Use Flashbacks without Slowing the Story

Flashbacks can be one of the most powerful storytelling tools in your thriller—but only if you know how to use them. Handled the wrong way, they kill your pacing, yank your reader out of the action, and dump a pile of backstory right when the tension is about to explode. But when used well, flashbacks can deepen character, add mystery, and create emotional stakes without slowing down the ride.

When you're writing your thriller in one day, you don't have time to get stuck in a backstory swamp. So, let's break down how to use flashbacks quickly, effectively, and surgically—so they serve your story without derailing it.

First, let's be clear: in a thriller, readers want to move forward. They want momentum. They want tension, action, and the desperate need to know what happens next. If you drag them backward too often or for too long, you'll break that momentum and risk losing them.

So, the golden rule of flashbacks in a thriller is simple: **keep them short, sharp, and story-critical.**

Every flashback should:

- Reveal something the protagonist needs to understand right now.
- Change how the reader interprets what's happening.
- Add emotional weight to the current action.
- Raise the stakes or tension.

If the flashback doesn't do one or more of these things, cut it.

You can use ChatGPT to help you structure this quickly. Prompt, **"What crucial backstory detail could I reveal through a short flashback in this thriller?"**

A common mistake writers make is using flashbacks to dump exposition. Instead of weaving backstory naturally into the present-day action, they stop the story cold and show the protagonist's entire childhood, failed marriage, or police training. That's not a flashback—that's an information dump disguised as a memory.

In a thriller, flashbacks should feel like **memories that hit hard and fast**, triggered by something happening in the present.

For example:

He watched the security footage loop again and again. The man's face half-hidden by shadows—but it was the scar above the eyebrow that froze him.

Fifteen years ago, in a hotel room in Marseille, that same scar had smiled at him over a loaded pistol.

That's all you need. Two sentences, and suddenly the protagonist's past and present collide. No long, dreamy fade-in scene required.

When writing fast, another great trick is to tie your flashbacks to **sensory triggers**. A sound, a smell, a place, a phrase—all can spark a quick, visceral memory. This makes the flashback feel natural and earned, not like the writer hit pause.

You can ask ChatGPT, **"What sensory triggers could remind the protagonist of a buried memory in this thriller?"**

Another thing that works beautifully in thrillers is using flashbacks to **mislead.**

You can show a flashback that makes the reader think they understand a character's motivation—only to later reveal that the memory was incomplete, unreliable, or a deliberate misdirection.

For example, early in the story, you show a flashback of the protagonist's partner dying because of a bad call. The protagonist is haunted by guilt. But later, you reveal another flashback—this time showing the partner's betrayal, the reason for that bad call, and how it changes everything.

That's not just backstory—that's a weapon.

You can use ChatGPT to help map this out. Prompt, **"Outline how to use flashbacks to mislead the reader in a thriller story."**

Placement is another key factor. Don't open your thriller with a long flashback. Start with action, tension, danger—something that hooks the reader. Then, once they're invested, you can slip in flashbacks at carefully chosen moments:

- When the protagonist is forced to make a choice.
- When a discovery triggers a memory.
- When the stakes escalate and the protagonist's past influences their decision.
- Right before or after a major plot twist, adding emotional or narrative context.

You can also use **fragmented flashbacks**—short, scattered glimpses of something the protagonist has buried or forgotten, building toward a full reveal at the climax. This is especially powerful in psychological thrillers, where the protagonist's memory itself might be unreliable.

And here's a pro tip: flashbacks don't always have to be paragraphs of prose.

You can drop in quick lines, snippets of dialogue, or sensory impressions to hint at the past without pausing the action.

For example:

The sound of a child crying.

Gunfire in the distance.

Her brother's hand slipping from hers.

Three lines. No full scene. But suddenly, the reader feels the weight of the protagonist's past.

When you're writing your thriller fast, this approach saves you time and keeps your pacing tight. You can even use ChatGPT to write these quick memory snippets. Prompt, **"Write three short, haunting flashback lines for a protagonist haunted by a past mistake."**

Finally, make sure your flashbacks **pay off.**

Don't tease the reader with memories if they don't change the story. Each flashback should add a piece to the puzzle, reveal a motivation, or twist the narrative. When you hit the climax, the reader should look back at those flashbacks and realize how they shaped everything.

In short, flashbacks in a thriller are like knives—you use them carefully, precisely, and for maximum impact. Done well, they don't slow your story down. They sharpen it.

Writing Multi-Perspective Thriller Narratives

If you want to level up your thriller and make it feel bigger, sharper, and more dynamic, one of the best storytelling tools you can use is a **multi-perspective narrative**. Instead of locking your story into one character's viewpoint, you tell it through the eyes of several characters—each with their own agenda, secrets, and fears. This isn't just a fancy writing technique; it's a structural weapon that lets you layer tension, mislead the reader, and keep the pace flying without sacrificing character depth.

And the best part? When you're writing a thriller in one day, multi-perspective storytelling can help you move faster, not slower—if you know how to do it right.

So, how does it work?

At its simplest, a multi-perspective thriller narrative means you're telling the story from more than one point of view. This could mean alternating between:

- **The protagonist and the antagonist.**
- **The investigator and the criminal.**
- **A key witness, a victim, or an unwitting pawn in the bigger game.**
- **An inside source or double agent.**

You can use ChatGPT to help you structure this quickly. Prompt, **"Outline a thriller plot with three key point-of-view characters."**

The biggest reason to use multiple perspectives is to build **tension and dramatic irony.**

When the reader knows something the protagonist doesn't, the tension skyrockets. If we see the villain laying a trap in one chapter, and then watch the protagonist walk straight into it in the next, the reader can't stop turning the pages.

It also allows you to show the **bigger picture**.

In a single-perspective thriller, you're limited to what the protagonist sees and knows. But when you widen the lens, you can show what's happening behind the scenes. The corporate boardroom. The antagonist's secret lair. The police investigation closing in. This gives your story scope and scale without slowing down the pace.

When writing fast, the easiest structure is to **alternate chapters** between viewpoints. Keep each chapter short and focused—think of them like cliffhangers that bounce the reader from one tense situation to the next.

But here's the key:

Each perspective should feel **necessary.**

Don't switch viewpoints just because you can. Each character's perspective should:

- Reveal something the others don't know.
- Offer emotional or psychological insight.
- Raise the stakes.
- Add tension, misdirection, or depth.

If a perspective isn't doing one of these things, cut it.

You can use ChatGPT to keep track of this. Prompt, **"For each POV character in this thriller, list what information only they can reveal."**

Another advantage of multi-perspective storytelling is that it allows you to **play with trust and misdirection.**

You can make one character an unreliable narrator. You can show how two characters interpret the same event differently. You can let the reader build assumptions based on one perspective—then flip everything by showing the same event from another angle.

For example: Chapter One: The protagonist believes they narrowly escaped a trap. Chapter Two: The antagonist's perspective reveals they let the protagonist escape—for a reason.

That kind of back-and-forth keeps the reader guessing and turns every chapter into a new piece of the puzzle.

Voice is another important factor.

Each perspective should feel distinct. This isn't about gimmicky accents or over-the-top style, but about mindset and worldview. Your protagonist might be tense, analytical, and determined. Your antagonist might be cold, arrogant, or emotionally detached. A supporting character might be nervous, impulsive, or unreliable.

You can use ChatGPT to help you shape this quickly. Prompt, **"Write a short internal monologue in the distinct voice of this thriller character."**

When you're writing fast, the risk with multiple perspectives is getting tangled in too many storylines. Keep it simple.

Three perspectives is usually the sweet spot. More than that, and your pacing might suffer unless you're very disciplined.

And when you switch perspectives, always leave the previous character's chapter on a hook. A cliffhanger. A question. A threat. Something that forces the reader to keep going because they need to know what happens next.

Another powerful technique is to **limit what each character knows.**

This creates natural tension. Maybe your protagonist is hunting the antagonist, but the reader knows from the villain's chapters that they're being manipulated. Maybe a supporting character knows a crucial piece of information, but the protagonist won't learn it until it's almost too late.

You can map this out with ChatGPT. Prompt, **"Create a chart showing what information each POV character knows in this thriller."**

You can also use multi-perspective storytelling to explore your **theme**.

If your thriller is about trust, show how each character struggles with who to trust. If it's about obsession, show how different characters' obsessions collide. This makes your thriller feel cohesive and layered.

Here's one more pro tip:

If you want to crank up the tension even further, let your perspectives **converge at the climax.**

All those separate threads and viewpoints should crash together in the final act. The protagonist finally meets the antagonist face to face. The supporting character's secret is revealed. The perspectives collapse into one final, breathless confrontation.

When done well, multi-perspective storytelling doesn't slow your thriller down—it makes it tighter, sharper, and more intense. It gives your reader no choice but to keep turning the pages, desperate to see how all the threads come together.

Writing Technology, Espionage, and Cyber Thrillers

There's something uniquely thrilling about stories that deal in the shadows of the digital world and global espionage. Technology, hacking, spies, surveillance, digital warfare—it's the stuff of modern nightmares and adrenaline-fueled thrillers. And when you're writing your thriller in one day, tapping into the world of **technology, espionage, and cybercrime** is one of the fastest ways to make your story feel urgent, modern, and frighteningly possible.

These kinds of thrillers are built on paranoia, secrecy, betrayal, and the terrifying realization that you're always being watched. They take the theme of control and strip it away from the protagonist, leaving them running from forces they can't even see.

So, how do you write one effectively—and fast?

Start with the core ingredients:

Technology + Power + Secrets + Stakes.

Whether it's stolen data, a government surveillance program, a cyber-attack, or a whistleblower on the run, the heart of a good tech-espionage thriller is something digital, intangible, and dangerous falling into the wrong hands.

When writing quickly, start by asking:

- What is the **threatening piece of technology**?
- Who wants it—and why?
- What will happen if they get it?
- How does the protagonist get caught in the middle?

You can use ChatGPT to help you generate this fast. Prompt, **"Create a cyber thriller premise involving espionage, stolen data, and high stakes."**

Here's an example: The protagonist is a freelance cybersecurity expert who accidentally intercepts a data packet revealing a global surveillance conspiracy. Suddenly, they're being hunted by international intelligence agencies, rogue hackers, and corporate hitmen—all trying to silence them before the truth gets out.

That's your ticking clock. That's your tension.

The next step is to decide how much of the **technical details** you want to show.

Cyber thrillers walk a fine line—you want to sound authentic, but you don't want to drown the reader in jargon or spend pages explaining how an algorithm works. The average reader doesn't care how encryption functions—they care about what's at stake if the protagonist can't break it.

So, when writing fast, focus on the **effects of the technology, not the mechanics.**

Instead of:

The AES-256 bit encryption protocol was nearly impossible to crack without the specific key...

Write:

The files were locked behind an impenetrable wall—and if he couldn't crack it before sunrise, thousands of lives would be at risk.

You can always use ChatGPT to simplify the language. Prompt, **"Explain this technical detail in plain language for a cyber thriller audience."**

Another major piece of this genre is **espionage.**

Cyber thrillers often overlap with spy thrillers because the digital world and the intelligence world go hand-in-hand. Hackers, whistle-blowers, spies, black-ops teams—all of them fighting over information instead of weapons.

When building your espionage layer quickly, focus on:

- **Mistrust and betrayal:** Who's double-crossing whom?
- **Layers of secrecy:** What's the real goal behind the mission?
- **Morally gray characters:** No one's hands are clean in espionage.

Your protagonist doesn't have to be a traditional spy. They could be an average person dragged into the world of cyber warfare. They could be a hacker, a journalist, a whistleblower, or even an ex-operative trying to stay out of the game.

You can use ChatGPT to help you flesh this out. Prompt, **"Create a morally ambiguous spy character for a cyber thriller."**

Another crucial piece of the cyber thriller puzzle is the **global scope.**

Technology knows no borders. Your story can—and should—jump from Moscow to London to Singapore to New York in a matter of pages. This keeps the pace fast and the stakes massive.

When writing quickly, use location shifts to **raise the stakes.**

Every time your protagonist moves to a new city or country, the threat should escalate:

- New enemies.
- Fewer allies.
- Higher consequences.
- A narrowing clock.

And don't forget about the **faceless threat.**

Cyber thrillers are unique because the danger often isn't a person—it's a system, an algorithm, a conspiracy buried behind firewalls and proxies. Your protagonist might never see the person pulling the strings until the very end.

That doesn't mean the antagonist is weak—it means they're everywhere and nowhere at once. And that's terrifying.

Another tool you can use is to let your protagonist's **personal life collide with the tech world.**

Maybe their family is being used as leverage. Maybe they're haunted by something they did in their past work. Maybe the data they're fighting over contains secrets about themselves.

This emotional connection grounds the technology in something human, which is crucial when the stakes are digital and abstract.

You can ask ChatGPT, **"Suggest ways to tie the protagonist's personal life into the cyber thriller's main conflict."**

And finally—don't forget the pacing.

Cyber thrillers should move fast. Short chapters. Tense scenes. Constant reveals, betrayals, and reversals. Let the reader feel the speed of the digital world reflected in the storytelling itself.

In your climax, make sure the final confrontation is both digital and personal. Maybe the protagonist finally faces the mastermind behind the conspiracy. Maybe they have to choose between leaking the truth or protecting someone they love. Maybe they realize the real threat wasn't the data—it was what they became to protect it.

When you're writing a thriller in one day, technology and espionage are your best friends. They let you create high stakes, global tension, and morally gray characters without needing to invent an entire fantasy world. And with ChatGPT in your toolkit, you can fill in the technical details fast, leaving you free to focus on the tension, twists, and character arcs.

How to Keep the Thriller Grounded and Believable

One of the fastest ways to lose a reader in a thriller is to let the story spiral into something so over-the-top, so ridiculous, or so unbelievable that they roll their eyes and stop caring. Thrillers are supposed to be thrilling, but if you want your story to stick, it has to feel like it **could actually happen**—or at least that it could almost happen.

Even when you're writing a thriller in one day, grounding your story in realism is what keeps the reader hooked and emotionally invested. Because no matter how wild the plot gets, readers will only stay on the ride if they **believe in the people and the world you've built.**

So how do you keep your thriller grounded while still delivering heart-pounding action and shocking twists?

First, start with your **characters.**

Characters are the anchor that keeps your story believable. No matter how big your plot is—whether it's a global cyber-attack, a serial killer on the loose, or a high-stakes political conspiracy—your characters should feel real, flawed, and human.

That means giving them realistic fears, desires, and weaknesses. Your protagonist shouldn't be superhuman. Let them get scared. Let them mess up. Let them question themselves. Readers want to root for someone who feels like a person, not a movie star stunt double.

You can use ChatGPT to help you build these layers quickly. Prompt, **"List realistic character flaws for a thriller protagonist."**

The same goes for your antagonist.

Even if your villain is powerful, dangerous, or brilliant, their actions and motives should feel plausible. Why are they doing what they're doing? What's their goal? What's their flaw? A believable antagonist isn't evil for evil's sake—they believe they're right, or they're driven by something understandable, even if it's twisted.

Another way to keep your thriller grounded is to build a **plausible plot.**

This doesn't mean your story has to be simple or boring. It means the chain of events should feel logical. Cause and effect should matter. When a character makes a decision, the consequences should follow naturally—even if they're unexpected.

Avoid plot conveniences or magical solutions. If your protagonist escapes danger, it should be because of their skills, quick thinking, or help from a believable source—not because a helicopter randomly appeared at the right moment.

When writing fast, you can use ChatGPT to check for plausibility. Prompt, **"Does this thriller plot have any unrealistic or illogical events?"** and let the AI help you spot potential holes.

Setting is another tool you can use to ground your story.

Readers will buy into wild plot twists if the world around them feels real. Describe settings with concrete, sensory details. The smell of wet concrete in an alley. The sound of traffic outside a safe house. The cold, sterile light of a hospital corridor. These small touches make your world feel lived-in, even when the stakes are high.

You can also use real-world locations, technologies, and procedures to add authenticity. If your story involves police work, get the basics right. If it involves cybercrime, use terminology accurately. You don't have to be an expert—just get the general framework correct so readers trust you.

ChatGPT is a huge time-saver here. Prompt, **"Summarize how a missing person investigation works"** or **"List real-world surveillance technologies used by intelligence agencies."**

One of the most effective ways to keep a thriller believable is to lean into **emotional realism.**

No matter how crazy the plot gets, readers will stay invested if the emotions feel real. Show how the protagonist's choices affect them. Show their fear, guilt, anger, and hope. Let them struggle with impossible choices. Let the cost of their actions weigh on them.

For example, if your protagonist is forced to betray a friend to stop a greater threat, don't just move past it. Show how it haunts them. That emotional fallout is what keeps the story grounded.

Another trick is to keep the **stakes personal.**

Even if your thriller involves global conspiracies or mass danger, make sure the protagonist has something personal at risk—a loved one, their freedom, their sanity. Big-picture stakes can feel abstract. Personal stakes make the tension real.

Also, watch out for **action overload.**

It's tempting to stack chase scenes, shootouts, and explosions to keep the reader entertained—but too much action without breathing space can make the story feel cartoonish. Balance action with quieter moments of tension, character development, and emotional fallout.

You can use ChatGPT to help pace this. Prompt, **"Outline a thriller story structure that balances action and character moments."**

Finally, avoid the temptation to solve everything with a **plot twist that breaks logic.**

Readers love a good twist—but they'll hate one that comes out of nowhere or ignores everything that came before. A believable twist feels inevitable in hindsight. It should make the reader say, **"Of course! How did I miss that?"** not, **"That makes no sense."**

Use foreshadowing. Plant clues. Keep your world consistent.

When you're writing your thriller in one day, it's easy to fall into the trap of over-the-top solutions because they're quick and exciting. But if you take the extra minute to ask yourself, **"Would this really happen?" or "Would this character really do this?"**, your story will feel sharper, smarter, and more grounded.

Your reader will trust you—and that trust is what keeps them turning pages.

Building and Maintaining Creative Control with ChatGPT

When you're writing a thriller in one day, especially using ChatGPT to help you, it's easy to fall into the trap of thinking the AI is doing the writing and you're just along for the ride. But here's the thing: ChatGPT is a tool, not a storyteller. **You are the creative engine.** You're the one who brings the voice, the emotion, the tension, and the meaning. The AI can only follow the lead you give it.

So, if you want to write a gripping, authentic, and personal thriller, you need to learn how to build and maintain **creative control** while using ChatGPT to do the heavy lifting.

Let's break down how you do that.

The first thing you need to remember is that **ChatGPT will write whatever you tell it to write.** It doesn't know your voice, your preferences, or the exact tone you want—unless you make it clear. That's why the most important part of writing a thriller with ChatGPT is knowing what you want before you start typing prompts.

The fastest way to lose creative control is to start throwing random requests at the AI and stitching together whatever it spits out. That's not writing—that's copy-paste chaos. Instead, approach your writing session like a director working with a talented assistant. You have the vision. ChatGPT is there to help execute it.

Start by defining the **core of your thriller.**

You can do this quickly with prompts like:

- **"Summarize the core conflict of this thriller in one sentence."**
- **"Describe the protagonist's flaw and goal."**
- **"What is the main theme driving this thriller?"**

Once you're clear on your story's spine, everything you generate should serve that vision.

Another essential part of keeping creative control is **controlling the voice and style.**

You don't want your thriller to read like a generic AI-generated story. You want it to sound like you wrote it.

The good news is you can teach ChatGPT your style.

You can start by giving it specific instructions like:

- **"Write this scene in an informal, fast-paced, conversational style."**
- **"Make the dialogue tense and snappy."**
- **"Use short, sharp sentences to build suspense."**

You can even paste a paragraph you've written and tell ChatGPT, **"Match this writing style."**

That's how you keep your voice front and center.

Another risk when using ChatGPT is losing control of the **pacing and structure.**

AI can generate endless content, but that doesn't mean it's going to pace the story well. That's your job.

You need to be the one deciding:

- Where to put cliffhangers.
- When to slow down for character moments.
- When to hit the gas and raise the stakes.

You can use ChatGPT to help you outline this quickly. Prompt, **"Outline a three-act thriller structure with key turning points."** Then, as you generate scenes, always ask: **Does this move the story forward? Does it build tension? Does it fit the pacing plan?**

Another part of creative control is making sure your thriller doesn't become a **cliché collage.**

AI can fall back on predictable tropes if you're not careful. That's why you should be specific and intentional in your prompts.

Instead of saying: **"Write an action scene in a thriller."** Say: **"Write an action scene where the protagonist is trying to outrun a surveillance drone in a crowded Istanbul market, showing their resourcefulness and fear."**

That level of direction keeps you in charge of the creative choices.

You also want to use ChatGPT to help you **solve problems, not make them.**

If you're stuck on a plot hole, don't let the AI derail your story by generating random filler. Instead, ask it specific, creative questions like:

- **"What are three believable ways the protagonist could escape this situation without being unrealistic?"**
- **"What personal stakes could I add to this twist to make it hit harder?"**

This keeps the creative control in your hands and turns ChatGPT into the collaborator it should be.

One of the best ways to stay in control is to **edit aggressively.**

ChatGPT can help you write fast, but that doesn't mean everything it produces is gold. You need to read every scene, tweak every sentence, and make sure it sounds like you. That's what makes the difference between an AI-written draft and a gripping thriller written by you with AI assistance.

Here's a simple process you can follow:

1. Use ChatGPT to generate raw scenes, descriptions, or dialogue based on your clear instructions.
2. Read each section carefully and decide: **Does this sound like me? Does it fit my story?**
3. Edit, rewrite, and reshape as needed.
4. Keep checking your outline or plot summary to make sure the story is still following your plan.

You can even use ChatGPT to help you refine your draft. Prompt, **"Rewrite this scene to make the dialogue sharper and more suspenseful."** Or, **"Cut unnecessary words from this paragraph without losing tension."**

Finally, don't forget the most important part of creative control: **your instincts.**

You're the storyteller. You know when something feels right, when a twist hits, when a scene is dragging. Trust that instinct. ChatGPT can help you move faster, brainstorm ideas, and fill in details—but it can't feel the story the way you can.

When you learn how to use ChatGPT without letting it take over, you become faster, sharper, and more efficient—but you stay in charge. You can write an entire thriller in one day without losing your voice, your vision, or your creative spark.

Editing Your Thriller Story Quickly and Effectively

You've done it—you've written an entire thriller in one day. The adrenaline, the tension, the twists and turns are all there on the page. But before you breathe that sigh of relief and call it finished, there's one last step you can't skip: **editing**.

The truth is, first drafts—especially when written fast—are messy. And that's okay. What matters now is how you shape, tighten, and sharpen that raw draft into something clean, tense, and unputdownable. But when you're working fast, you can't afford to spend weeks fiddling with commas and cutting single words. You need a process that helps you edit quickly and effectively without draining your energy or momentum.

Here's how you do it.

The first thing to understand is that editing a thriller is not just about fixing typos. It's about **enhancing tension, tightening pace, clarifying stakes, and cutting anything that slows the story down**. So, your editing focus should be strategic, not mechanical.

Start with a **big-picture pass.**

Read your story like a reader, not a writer. Get a notebook or a fresh ChatGPT window open and take notes as you go. Don't worry about grammar yet. Ask yourself:

- Does the story make sense?
- Are the stakes clear?
- Does every chapter end with tension, a hook, or an unanswered question?
- Are there any slow parts where nothing important happens?
- Do the twists land? Or do they feel confusing or forced?

When you're writing fast, it's easy to lose track of structure. This is your chance to make sure the story flows, escalates, and delivers.

You can also use ChatGPT as your editing partner here. Prompt, **"Read this thriller story and identify any plot holes or confusing sections."** Paste sections at a time and let the AI help you spot problems you might miss when you're too close to the work.

Once you've made your big-picture notes, move to a **scene-level pass.**

Go chapter by chapter and ask:

- Is this scene necessary?
- Does it move the plot forward, develop character, or raise tension?
- Could it be tighter, shorter, or combined with another scene?

If a scene doesn't serve one of those purposes, cut it. Your thriller should move fast. Every scene should feel like a domino falling toward the climax.

Next, look at your **characters.**

When writing quickly, characters can sometimes drift out of focus or act inconsistently. Go back through and make sure:

- The protagonist's arc is clear. They should change, grow, or be broken by the end.
- The antagonist is believable and dangerous, not a cartoon.
- Supporting characters have clear roles and motivations.
- No character disappears without a reason.

Ask ChatGPT to help if needed. Prompt, **"Summarize this protagonist's character arc based on this story."** If the summary doesn't match what you intended, go back and tighten it.

Now it's time to edit for **pacing.**

Thrillers live and die by pace. So, go through each chapter and look for:

- Long, unnecessary exposition. Cut it.
- Overwritten descriptions. Trim them.
- Slow dialogue exchanges. Make them snappier.
- Action scenes that drag. Keep them sharp and clear.

You can use a simple trick here: **count the beats.**

If you have three paragraphs between a moment of tension and the next piece of action, cut it to one. Keep the reader breathless.

ChatGPT can help with this too. Prompt, **"Shorten this scene without losing tension."**

Once you've streamlined pacing, do a **dialogue pass.**

Good thriller dialogue is sharp, purposeful, and tense. Go through your conversations and cut:

- Small talk.
- Over-explaining.
- Lines that don't reveal character or raise stakes.

Dialogue is a great place to inject character and tension fast. Make every line do something important.

Next, tackle the **language level.**

This is where you polish sentences, tighten word choices, and make sure your writing has punch. Replace passive verbs with active ones. Cut unnecessary words. Make descriptions lean and vivid.

Instead of:

He was going to try to escape the room. Write: He lunged for the door.

You can prompt ChatGPT to help: **"Tighten this paragraph for clarity and pace."**

After that, do a **proofreading pass.**

This is the mechanical part. Grammar, spelling, punctuation, formatting. If you're writing in one day, you're going to have typos. That's fine. But clean them up now.

You can run your manuscript through a grammar checker—or even ask ChatGPT to help. Prompt, **"Check this paragraph for grammar and spelling mistakes."**

Finally, do a **read-aloud pass.**

This is one of the fastest and most effective ways to catch clunky sentences, awkward phrasing, or pacing issues. Read the entire manuscript aloud. Or, better yet, use text-to-speech software and listen to your story like an audiobook.

If anything makes you stumble or sounds off, fix it.

And here's the key to all of this: **Don't over-edit.**

The point of writing a thriller in one day is speed and momentum. Your story should be tight, fast, and raw in the best way. Don't edit the life out of it. Clean it, sharpen it, but don't polish it into something bland or overworked.

You can even give yourself a hard limit: **One editing pass per level.**

One big-picture pass. One scene-level pass. One dialogue pass. One proofreading pass. Done.

The goal isn't perfection. The goal is a thriller that **moves, hooks, and thrills.** A story that's clean enough to keep readers glued to the page but still carries the raw, beating heart of something written fast and on fire.

How to Create an Irresistible Thriller Book Title

You can write the most gripping, fast-paced, mind-bending thriller in the world—but if your book title doesn't hook the reader in one glance, you're already fighting an uphill battle. Your title is your first impression. It's the first spark of tension, curiosity, or intrigue your reader will feel before they even read the first page. And when you're writing a thriller in one day, you need a title that's sharp, clear, and makes a promise: **This story will keep you on the edge of your seat.**

So, how do you craft a killer thriller title quickly and effectively?

First, let's talk about what makes a great thriller title.

At its core, a strong thriller title does one or more of the following:

- Creates **mystery**: It makes the reader ask a question.
- Suggests **danger**: There's a sense of threat or tension baked in.
- Feels **specific**: It doesn't sound generic; it hints at your unique story.
- Is **punchy and memorable**: No long-winded, vague titles.
- Suggests **stakes** or urgency.

Think about famous thrillers: **The Girl with the Dragon Tattoo. The Da Vinci Code. Gone Girl. The Silent Patient. Before I Go to Sleep. The Bourne Identity.**

Each of those titles makes you curious. Each has a mystery or question built into it. And none of them waste words.

When you're writing fast, you can brainstorm your title alongside your story. In fact, sometimes knowing your title early can help you shape the plot and the tension. It becomes your north star.

So, let's break down some **title formulas** that work almost every time in the thriller genre.

One popular formula is: **The [Noun] + of + [Noun]** Examples: The Silence of the Lambs

The Shadow of Fear

The House of Lies

This structure is simple but effective. It suggests something ominous, mysterious, or dangerous.

Another classic is: **The [Adjective] + [Noun]** Examples: The Silent Patient

The Missing Sister

The Broken Code

The Dark Conspiracy

You can brainstorm your own in seconds. Try prompting ChatGPT:

"List thriller title ideas in the format 'The [Adjective] [Noun]' based on this story."

Then there's the **One-Word Title**—short, punchy, impactful: **Gone. Shattered. Betrayal. Hunted. Vanished.**

One-word titles work well when the word itself carries strong thriller energy. But they only work if the word is unique and relevant to your plot. Otherwise, they risk sounding generic.

Another title strategy is to use a **time limit or countdown: 24 Hours. The Final Day. Before Midnight. Countdown to Zero.**

If your thriller has a ticking clock, lean into it with your title. It immediately creates urgency.

You can also hint at the protagonist or antagonist's identity: **The Cleaner. The Double Agent. The Stranger Inside. The Widow's Game.**

This works well if your story revolves around a specific, mysterious figure.

Or you can make the title a question or statement that teases the plot: **Who Did It? No One is Safe. She Knows Too Much. Trust No One.**

These titles pull readers in because they hint at danger and betrayal.

When you're writing fast, you can use a simple brainstorming process:

1. Write down the core **theme** of your story.
2. Write down your protagonist and antagonist's defining traits.
3. Write down your story's biggest threat or mystery.
4. Write down any symbols, locations, or objects that matter.

Then mix and match.

For example, if your thriller is about a missing child and a corrupt corporation, your title might become:

The Missing Son

The Corporation's Secret

Before He's Gone

The Shadow Deal

You can also use ChatGPT to accelerate this process. Prompt:

"Suggest 20 thriller book titles based on a story about [brief description]."

Once you have a list, don't overthink. Pick the one that hits hardest, feels sharp, and instantly communicates danger, mystery, or tension.

A quick note about clichés:

Yes, thriller titles lean heavily on words like **Dark, Silent, Secret, Fear, Trust, Betrayal, Missing, Gone, Countdown, Game**—and for good reason. They work. They signal genre instantly. So don't be afraid to use them, but make sure your title has something personal or specific to your story that makes it stand out.

Finally, make sure your title is:

- **Easy to remember**
- **Easy to say out loud**
- **Easy to search for online**

Because a great title isn't just about storytelling—it's also about marketing. You want readers to see it, remember it, and feel a spark of curiosity every time they hear it.

So, as you wrap up writing your thriller in one day, spend an extra 10 minutes nailing down the title. It might seem like a small thing, but the right title is the hook that gets readers to stop scrolling, pick up your book, and dive into the world you've created.

In the next chapter, we'll talk about how to use your book description and first chapter to hook readers even further and make sure they can't put your thriller down once they've started.

Writing Your Thriller Book Description with ChatGPT

Once you've written and edited your thriller—whether you spent one day or one month on it—there's one last piece of writing that can make or break how many people actually read it: **the book description**. And here's what most writers won't tell you—writing the description is often harder than writing the book itself.

Because now you've got to distill all that tension, mystery, danger, and drama into a few sharp, snappy paragraphs that hook potential readers instantly. No fluff, no wasted words. This is your sales pitch. It's the back cover blurb. The bit readers see when they're scrolling online deciding whether to click "Buy Now" or scroll on by.

The good news? When you're writing a thriller in one day, you already have a huge advantage: You're in the zone. You know your story inside out. You know the stakes, the protagonist, the danger, and the hook. All you need is a clear, quick process to turn that knowledge into an irresistible book description.

And ChatGPT can help you do that fast.

Let's break it down.

The first thing to remember is that a thriller book description isn't a plot summary. You're not telling the entire story. You're teasing it. You're creating curiosity, tension, and urgency. You want the reader to ask one question when they finish reading your blurb: **What happens next?**

Most successful thriller descriptions follow a simple structure:

1. **Introduce the protagonist.** Who are they? Why should we care?
2. **Introduce the conflict.** What threat, danger, or mystery are they facing?
3. **Raise the stakes.** What's at risk if they fail?
4. **End with a hook.** A question, a cliffhanger, or a statement that demands the reader open the book.

Here's an example of that structure in action:

Former detective Sarah Blake thought she'd left the darkness behind—until a chilling message drags her back into a case she couldn't solve.

A young girl has vanished without a trace, and the only clue is a symbol left at the scene—a symbol Sarah has seen before.

As she races against time to find the missing child, Sarah uncovers a conspiracy that reaches further than she ever imagined.

The closer she gets, the more she realizes: this time, it's not just the girl's life on the line—it's her own.

Can she solve the puzzle before it's too late? Or will the shadows of the past finally catch up with her?

You can easily use ChatGPT to help you draft something like this. Prompt: **"Write a back cover thriller book description based on this plot: [Insert a one-paragraph summary of your thriller]."**

But don't stop there.

Once ChatGPT gives you a draft, read it out loud. Does it sound punchy? Does it tease the right details? Does it make you want to turn the page? If not, tweak it. Cut the fat. Make the language sharper.

Here's a tip: **Every sentence should be pulling the reader forward.**

If you find yourself explaining too much or giving away too many plot points, pull back. Mystery sells in a thriller description. You want to reveal enough to hook the reader but leave them desperate to know more.

You can also try multiple versions.

Ask ChatGPT: **"Write three versions of this thriller book description: one short and snappy, one dark and moody, and one focused on the protagonist's emotional journey."**

Then pick the one that hits hardest—or combine the best lines from each.

Another thing to watch for is **genre signals.**

Your description should clearly tell the reader this is a thriller. You do that with word choice:

- Words like **danger, secrets, race against time, shocking, chilling, deadly, betrayal, conspiracy, hunted, unstoppable, twisted.**
- Short, punchy sentences that create urgency.
- A clear threat or mystery.

If your description sounds like it could belong to a romance or a fantasy story, tighten it up. Readers of thrillers want tension and danger—you need to give them that feeling in the description.

Once you have a solid draft, test it.

Show it to a few people (or even run it past ChatGPT) and ask: **"Does this description make you want to read the book? If not, why?"**

Sometimes fresh eyes can spot when you're giving away too much—or not enough.

Finally, don't overthink it.

When you're writing a thriller in one day, you don't need a Pulitzer-worthy book blurb. You need a clear, clean, tension-filled teaser that tells readers: **This story will keep you up all night.**

Here's a simple checklist you can use to finish your description quickly:

- Have I introduced the protagonist?
- Have I introduced the conflict or threat?
- Have I raised the stakes?
- Have I ended with a hook?
- Does the language create tension and urgency?
- Is it under 200 words (so it fits well on a sales page)?

Once you can answer yes to all of those, you're done.

Turning Your Thriller into a Series

You've just finished writing your thriller in one day. It's got action, tension, twists, and a killer ending. But here's something you should be thinking about even before you type "The End"—**What's next?** Because the truth is, the best thrillers don't stop with one book. Readers love series. They love following a protagonist over multiple stories, watching them grow, struggle, and face new dangers. And if you want to turn your one-day thriller into something bigger, building a series is the smartest move you can make.

So, how do you do it?

First, let's be clear: **You don't need to plan a massive, sprawling saga from the start.**

You just need to leave the door open. Think of your first book as **Book One**—a self-contained, satisfying story that also hints at bigger things to come.

The best way to do this is to make sure your protagonist's journey isn't completely finished at the end of Book One. Sure, they solve the mystery, stop the bad guy, or save the day—but what's the cost? What wounds do they carry? What questions are left unanswered?

That's your starting point for a series.

When you're writing fast, here's a simple method to build a series structure:

1. Make your protagonist **compelling and complex.**
   Someone readers want to follow. Someone with flaws, trauma, unfinished business. Readers don't just come back for the plot—they come back for the character.
2. Create a **world or setting** that's rich enough for more than one story.
   A police department. A spy network. A small town full of secrets. A global conspiracy.
   If your world feels alive, you'll always have more stories to tell.
3. Design a **series arc.**
   Each book should have its own standalone story—its own beginning, middle, and end—but there should also be a bigger narrative threading through the books. A mystery that's not fully solved. A villain who escapes. A personal question that haunts the protagonist.

You can use ChatGPT to help map this quickly. Prompt, **"Outline a three-book thriller series arc based on this story."**

Another option is to write a **character-driven series** instead of a plot-driven one.

Think of Jack Reacher, Harry Bosch, or Lisbeth Salander. Each book has a new case, a new threat—but it's the character that ties the series together. Their world, their relationships, their inner struggles.

If you're writing in this style, you can ask ChatGPT, **"Suggest five standalone thriller plots for this protagonist."**

A powerful tool to keep readers coming back is the **unresolved thread.**

At the end of Book One, leave something lingering. Maybe it's a side character who disappears. Maybe it's a secret the protagonist uncovers but doesn't fully understand. Maybe it's a new threat emerging in the final pages.

You can even end with a subtle tease:

He thought it was over.

Until the phone rang again.

That's how you hook readers for Book Two without leaving them feeling cheated.

When you're planning your series, think about how your protagonist will **change over time.**

In Book One, maybe they're haunted by their past. In Book Two, they're trying to trust again. In Book Three, they're finally forced to confront the demons they've been running from.

That's what makes a thriller series addictive.

The reader isn't just following the plot—they're watching the protagonist evolve.

You can use ChatGPT to speed this up. Prompt, **"Outline the protagonist's emotional arc across a three-book thriller series."**

Another benefit of turning your thriller into a series is that it simplifies your writing process. Once you've built the world, the characters, and the tone, the next book is easier. You're not starting from scratch—you're building on what you've already created.

When you're writing fast, that's gold.

You can also build a series by expanding your **cast of characters.**

Side characters who played small roles in Book One can take center stage in later books. The cop, the hacker, the ex-partner, the journalist—all can become protagonists of their own stories, set in the same world.

This gives you endless storytelling potential without having to reinvent the wheel.

You can even prompt ChatGPT:

"Suggest a spin-off thriller plot based on this supporting character."

And don't underestimate the **marketing power** of a series.

Readers who love Book One are more likely to buy Book Two, Three, Four, and beyond. Series sell. And when you're writing thrillers quickly, you can keep that momentum going and build a backlist of gripping, connected stories that feed each other.

A practical tip:

When you publish or share Book One, include a **tease for the next book** at the end. A sample chapter, a title, a "coming soon" note. Keep your readers hungry.

In short, turning your thriller into a series isn't just smart storytelling—it's smart strategy.

It gives you creative momentum, builds an audience, and lets you spend more time with the characters and world you've worked so hard to create.

Using ChatGPT to Brainstorm Book Covers and Marketing Ideas

Writing a thriller in one day is an incredible accomplishment—but once the story is done, the real game begins. Because no matter how thrilling, fast-paced, and brilliant your book is, readers won't even open it if the **cover doesn't grab them** and they don't know it exists. That's where marketing comes in. And just like you used ChatGPT to write your thriller, you can use it to help you brainstorm cover concepts and marketing strategies quickly and effectively.

Let's start with the book cover.

The first rule of thriller book covers is simple: **It has to look like a thriller.**

Readers need to glance at your cover and immediately know what kind of story they're getting. That means dark colors, bold fonts, strong imagery, and a sense of mystery or danger.

But how do you come up with a good cover idea fast?

You can start by identifying three things:

1. **Your story's main symbol or motif.** Is there an object, place, or image central to your story? A red file, a burning photograph, a dark alley, a weapon, a missing person's photo?
2. **Your protagonist or antagonist.** Sometimes the cover hints at a key character—a silhouette, a face in shadow, someone running.
3. **Your setting or atmosphere.** A foggy city street. A cold mountain range. A darkened surveillance room.

Once you've listed a few options, you can jump over to ChatGPT and prompt: **"Suggest 10 thriller book cover concepts based on this story: [Brief description]."**

ChatGPT will give you solid, specific ideas like:

- A lone figure running across a bridge at night, city skyline in the background.
- A close-up of a gloved hand holding a USB drive dripping with blood.
- A dark alley with a flickering neon sign and a shadow disappearing around a corner.

You can then take these ideas to a designer, an AI image tool, or a cover-making app and start experimenting.

When you're working fast, you can even ask ChatGPT to suggest a **color palette** and **font style** that matches thriller genre conventions. Prompt: **"Suggest a color scheme and typography style for a fast-paced modern thriller book."**

Once your cover is in progress, you'll want to shift to **marketing ideas**—and yes, ChatGPT can help you move fast here too.

Think of your book marketing in three categories:

1. **How to get attention.**
2. **How to hook potential readers.**
3. **How to keep readers engaged and turn them into fans.**

You can start by asking ChatGPT: **"List 10 ways to market a thriller book online."**

It will give you classic suggestions like:

- Create a suspenseful book trailer.
- Share teaser excerpts on social media.
- Run a free promo on Kindle for 3 days.
- Reach out to thriller book bloggers and reviewers.
- Join Facebook groups and subreddits for thriller readers.
- Use targeted ads on Amazon or Facebook.
- Build an email list and offer a free short thriller as a signup incentive.
- Post behind-the-scenes content about how you wrote the book in one day.
- Use cliffhanger snippets as Twitter or Instagram hooks.
- Host a Q&A session or live reading online.

You can take it even further and ask ChatGPT for specific content: **"Write five social media posts to promote my thriller book."**

"Draft a short, suspenseful email to announce my new thriller release."

"Write a sample blog post about how I wrote a thriller in one day using ChatGPT."

You can also brainstorm **taglines** and marketing hooks with ChatGPT.

Prompt: **"Suggest 10 tagline ideas for a thriller book about a missing child and a detective racing against time."**

These taglines are crucial when designing ads, social media posts, or even the back cover.

Another marketing angle you can lean into is the fact that you wrote the book **in one day with AI assistance.** That's a hook in itself. People are curious about how fast books can be written, and readers, bloggers, and indie publishing communities will be intrigued.

You can use this to craft marketing content like:

- **Blog post:** "How I Wrote a Gripping Thriller in One Day with ChatGPT"
- **Social post:** "What if I told you this entire thriller novel was written in 24 hours? Here's how."
- **Reader challenge:** "Can you spot the AI-written twist in my new thriller?"

By turning the process itself into part of your marketing story, you'll stand out from the sea of thrillers competing for attention.

And don't forget about building a long-term strategy.

If you're following this book's advice and planning to turn your thriller into a **series**, you can start teasing Book Two in your marketing even before it's written. Readers love knowing there's more to come.

You can ask ChatGPT to help you plan this: **"Outline a marketing campaign for a three-book thriller series."**

The key to effective marketing is consistency and speed—both of which you can achieve using AI to help you generate content ideas, outlines, captions, blurbs, and promotional copy in minutes rather than hours.

And remember: Marketing doesn't stop when you publish your book.

Your cover, blurb, tagline, social media posts, emails, and even the first few pages of your book all work together to keep pulling readers in.

How to Avoid Clichés and Overused Tropes

Thrillers are one of the most popular genres in the world—and with that popularity comes a problem: over time, certain tropes, characters, and plot devices get recycled so often that they lose their punch. Readers see them coming a mile away. And nothing kills suspense faster than predictability.

When you're writing a thriller in one day with ChatGPT, it's easy to lean on familiar clichés because they're fast and recognizable. But if you want your thriller to stand out and actually thrill readers, you need to recognize those tired tropes—and learn how to flip, twist, or avoid them.

So, let's talk about how to dodge the most common traps and keep your story fresh.

First, let's get something clear. **Tropes aren't bad.**

Tropes are just patterns and tools in storytelling. The problem isn't the trope itself—it's when it's used lazily, predictably, or without adding anything new.

Take the classic thriller trope:

"The hero has nothing left to lose."

It's not bad on its own. A broken, desperate protagonist can be compelling. But if they're the same hard-drinking, emotionally shut-off ex-cop we've seen in a hundred other thrillers, readers will tune out.

Your job is to take the expected and make it unexpected.

So how do you do that quickly and effectively?

Start by **knowing the clichés.**

Here are a few of the most overused thriller tropes:

- The alcoholic detective haunted by a tragic past.
- The "one last job" storyline.
- The villain who reveals the entire plan before killing the hero.
- The twist where the protagonist's best friend/partner was the bad guy all along.
- The "it was all a dream" ending.
- A female character who only exists to be kidnapped or killed to motivate the male hero.
- Endless chase scenes that don't move the plot forward.
- Perfectly timed last-minute rescues.

When you're writing fast, it's tempting to grab one of these familiar pieces and drop it in. Don't.

Instead, use ChatGPT as a brainstorming partner to help you flip the cliché. Prompt: **"List ways to subvert the 'hard-drinking ex-cop' trope in a thriller."**

Or:

"Give me unexpected twists on the 'double agent' trope."

Another method is to look for **character clichés** and deliberately make the opposite choice.

If the obvious move is to make your hero a loner with nothing to lose, try making them a happily married teacher who stumbles into danger and has everything to lose. If the typical hacker in a cyber-thriller is a snarky, hoodie-wearing twenty-something, try making them a middle-aged mom or a retired school principal.

Fresh characters = fresh tension.

Next, look at your **plot twists.**

Readers of thrillers are smart. They've seen it all. So, if you're going to drop a twist, it needs to be:

- **Earned:** The clues were there.
- **Unpredictable:** But still believable.
- **Character-driven:** Not just a gimmick.

Avoid twists that only exist to shock the reader but don't change the story meaningfully. Instead, build twists that make the reader want to go back and re-read everything leading up to it.

You can use ChatGPT to help here. Prompt: **"Suggest three unexpected but believable twists for this thriller plot."**

Another cliché to watch out for is the **"invincible hero" syndrome.**

If your protagonist survives every explosion, gunfight, and betrayal without real consequences, the tension disappears. Readers know nothing bad will happen.

Instead, make the danger real. Let your hero fail, bleed, lose people they care about, question themselves. That's what makes the stakes feel high.

Also, be careful with **villains.**

The moustache-twirling, "evil for evil's sake" villain is tired. Real villains believe they're right. Give your antagonist real motivation, and if you can, let the reader understand or even sympathize with them.

When writing fast, you can prompt ChatGPT:

"Help me develop a morally complex antagonist for this thriller."

Dialogue clichés are another danger zone.

Lines like:

"We're not so different, you and I." "There's no time to explain!" "You'll never get away with this!"

They're cheesy, overused, and pull readers out of the story.

Instead, write dialogue that sounds real, tense, and sharp. Let characters speak like people—not stock movie lines.

You can ask ChatGPT to help tighten dialogue:

"Rewrite this dialogue to sound fresh and tense without clichés."

Setting clichés can creep in, too.

The abandoned warehouse, the dark alley, the rain-soaked rooftop. These aren't bad settings—but if they're the same ones every thriller uses, find a way to make them new.

Set your final confrontation in a brightly lit, crowded supermarket. Or in the middle of a children's birthday party. Or in a quiet library. Flip the expectation.

You can prompt ChatGPT:

"Suggest unusual settings for a tense confrontation scene in a thriller."

Finally, keep an eye on **plot convenience.**

If the hero's escape, discovery, or survival depends on pure coincidence or a ridiculous stroke of luck, your readers will feel cheated. Make sure the tension comes from your protagonist's choices, skills, and flaws—not from lazy plotting.

When you're writing your thriller in one day, it's easy to grab whatever solution is fastest. That's fine in your first draft—but when you edit, look for places where the story feels too easy, too obvious, too "seen it before." Then fix it.

Here's the good news:

Avoiding clichés doesn't mean you have to reinvent the genre. Readers love thrillers because they deliver certain promises—danger, twists, tension. Your job is to deliver those promises in a way that feels fresh, sharp, and real.

And the fastest way to do that? Keep asking yourself and ChatGPT: **What's the unexpected choice here?**

How can I flip this familiar trope?

What would surprise the reader—but still make sense?

If you follow that rule, you won't just write a thriller in one day. You'll write one that feels like it took months to craft.

Self-Publishing Your Thriller Story in One Day

You've done it. You've written your thriller. It's sharp, fast, tense, and gripping. You've edited it. You've brainstormed your title, crafted your book description, and even thought about turning it into a series. But now comes the step where most writers freeze: **Getting it out into the world.**

The good news is that thanks to modern publishing platforms, you can now go from a finished manuscript to a published thriller **in the same day**—and ChatGPT can help you every step of the way.

So, let's walk through exactly how to self-publish your thriller story quickly and efficiently without losing your mind.

The first step is choosing your **publishing platform.**

If you want speed, reach, and simplicity, your best option is **Amazon Kindle Direct Publishing (KDP).**

KDP allows you to publish your thriller as an eBook and a paperback with zero upfront cost. It's the biggest marketplace in the world for self-published thrillers, and your book will appear on Amazon within 24-48 hours after uploading (often much faster for eBooks).

If you want to go beyond Amazon, you can also use platforms like **Draft2Digital, Smashwords, or Kobo Writing Life** to distribute your book to Apple Books, Barnes & Noble, Google Play, and more. But if you're aiming to publish in one day, start with KDP—it's streamlined, reliable, and fast.

Next, you'll need to prepare your **manuscript file.**

KDP accepts Word documents (.doc or .docx), PDF, or ePub files. The easiest way to format your thriller manuscript quickly is to use a simple, clean Word template.

Here's what you need to check:

- Clear chapter headings.
- Consistent font (11 or 12pt, Times New Roman or Garamond works well).
- No fancy graphics or fonts that won't translate to Kindle.
- Paragraphs properly aligned and spaced.

You can even ask ChatGPT to help you format the chapters: **"Format this thriller manuscript in KDP-friendly style."**

Once your manuscript is ready, you'll need to design your **book cover.**

You've already brainstormed ideas in Chapter 59, so now it's time to make it real.

You can use free, fast cover creation tools like:

- **Canva (with their Book Cover templates)**
- **BookBrush**
- **KDP's own Cover Creator tool**

Make sure your cover includes:

- A bold, readable title.
- Your name or pen name.
- A dark, tense, thriller vibe.
- Simplicity—don't overload it.

If you have the skills and time, you can even use an AI image generator to create background artwork and then add text with Canva.

Once your cover is ready, you're ready to upload.

Now, head to **kdp.amazon.com** and create your free account if you don't already have one.

You'll go through a three-step process: **1. Book Details**

Add your thriller title, subtitle (optional), book description (which you already wrote in Chapter 57), author name, and categories.

For categories, make sure you choose thriller-related ones like:

- Mystery & Thrillers → Crime Thrillers
- Mystery & Thrillers → Psychological Thrillers
- Mystery & Thrillers → Suspense

You'll also choose keywords here. Use ChatGPT to help you brainstorm: **"Suggest 7 search keywords for a thriller eBook about a missing person and a race against time."**

2. Content Upload

Upload your formatted manuscript file.

Upload your book cover.

Preview your book using the KDP Previewer tool to make sure everything looks good.

Choose if you want to enable Digital Rights Management (DRM) or not—most indie authors turn it off to make sharing easier.

3. Pricing and Publishing

Set your price. For a short, fast-paced thriller, $2.99 to $4.99 is the sweet spot.

Choose territories (you can publish worldwide with one click).

Decide whether to enroll in **KDP Select** (which gives you access to Kindle Unlimited but requires 90 days of Amazon exclusivity).

Click **Publish.**

That's it.

Your thriller will be live as an eBook within a few hours to 48 hours max. If you upload a paperback version, that can take a little longer to appear.

If you want to publish a paperback at the same time, KDP will guide you to upload a paperback manuscript (same interior file, formatted for print) and a print-ready cover.

And here's the best part:

You can keep using ChatGPT even after you hit publish.

Use it to:

- Write your Amazon Author Bio.
- Draft your "About the Author" page at the end of the book.
- Brainstorm promotional emails and social media posts.
- Create a launch plan for your thriller series.

You can even ask: **"Write a one-week marketing plan for my newly published thriller eBook."**

Is publishing in one day perfect? No.

There will always be things you can fine-tune—cover polish, blurb tweaks, keyword optimization. But you don't have to wait until everything's "perfect" to hit publish.

Done is better than perfect. You can always go back and update your book on KDP anytime.

The point is, if you want to write, edit, package, and publish a thriller story in a single day—you can. You have the tools. You have the knowledge. And now, with this book and ChatGPT, you have a process.

So go write it. Go publish it.

Your readers are waiting.

Building a Readership for Your Thriller Stories

You've written your thriller. You've edited it. You've published it. You've even learned how to craft killer titles, book descriptions, and eye-catching covers. But now comes the real question—the one that every author, whether traditionally published or self-published, has to answer: **How do I get readers to actually read my book?**

The truth is, writing the book is just the beginning. If you want your thriller stories to reach people, you have to learn how to build a **readership.** You don't need to be a marketing expert. You don't need millions of followers or a giant advertising budget. You just need consistency, connection, and a strategy that plays to your strengths.

And, of course, you can use ChatGPT to help you speed up the process.

The first thing you need to understand is that **readers don't just stumble upon books anymore.**

They're being bombarded with choices every day. Hundreds of thrillers are published every single week. So, your job is to make sure that when a reader is looking for their next heart-pounding story, your book is right there in front of them—and when they finish it, they want more from you.

So, how do you start?

The best place is the most obvious: **The people who already read your book.**

Every time someone reads your thriller, you want to make it easy for them to stay connected to you. That's why your thriller should always end with a clear, friendly **Call to Action** like:

Loved this story? Get the next book in the series here: [Link]

Want exclusive bonus content and free thrillers? Join my Readers Club here: [Link]

This is the start of building your **email list**, which is still the single most powerful tool you can use to grow your readership.

Your email list is a direct line to people who want to hear from you. No algorithms. No gatekeepers. Just readers who've already said, "I want more."

You can use ChatGPT to help you write your email welcome sequence: **"Write a 3-part email welcome series for my thriller readers."**

Next, you need to be **where thriller readers hang out.**

That means:

- **Facebook groups** for thriller fans.
- **Goodreads thriller discussion boards.**
- **Subreddits like r/thrillers or r/books.**
- **BookTok and Bookstagram hashtags focused on crime, mystery, and thrillers.**
- **Thriller book review blogs and newsletters.**

But here's the key: Don't show up and immediately start shouting about your book. That's the fastest way to get ignored.

Instead, show up as a reader and a fan. Join conversations. Share book recommendations. Post interesting thriller trivia, movie comparisons, or writing insights.

You want readers to know you're part of the community—not just there to sell something.

You can use ChatGPT to help brainstorm social content. Prompt: **"Write 5 social media post ideas to engage thriller readers."**

Collaborating with other authors is another smart move.

Thriller authors aren't your competition—they're your allies. Reach out to other indie thriller writers and propose cross-promotions:

- Share each other's books in your email newsletters.
- Bundle your books in a discounted box set.
- Do joint giveaways.

Building relationships with other writers helps you tap into their audiences, too.

You can even ask ChatGPT: **"Draft an email proposal to another thriller author about cross-promoting our books."**

Another long-term strategy is to start building a **brand identity.**

What kind of thrillers do you write?

Are they gritty and violent? Psychological and twisty? Globetrotting espionage?

The clearer you are about your style, the easier it is to attract readers who will love your stories and keep coming back for more.

Make sure this identity is reflected everywhere:

- Your book covers.
- Your Amazon author page.
- Your website.
- Your social media profiles.

You can prompt ChatGPT: **"Help me write a personal author bio for my Amazon page, focusing on my thriller books."**

And remember—**one book isn't enough.**

The fastest way to build a readership is to keep publishing.

Readers love series. They love knowing that if they like one book, there's more waiting for them. So once you've published your first thriller, don't stop. Start writing the next one. Use the system you've built in this book to produce a steady stream of stories that feed into each other.

You don't need to be everywhere at once. You don't need to go viral.

You just need to show up consistently, write great stories, and make it easy for readers to find you, follow you, and keep reading.

Here's a simple, sustainable system you can build (and yes, ChatGPT can help you automate a lot of this):

1. Write and publish thrillers consistently.
2. End every book with an invite to join your email list or read the next book.
3. Engage in thriller reader communities online.
4. Share content, book recommendations, and behind-the-scenes insights.
5. Cross-promote with other thriller authors.
6. Keep refining your brand identity and author presence.

Before you know it, you'll have readers eagerly waiting for your next book—because you didn't just write a thriller.

You built a world they want to live in, and a name they want to follow.

And that's how you turn one day of writing into a lasting, growing readership.

Examples of Good Prompts for Story Design and Structure

One of the biggest advantages of using ChatGPT to write a thriller story in one day is how fast you can move through brainstorming, structuring, and writing—**if you know how to ask the right questions.** The quality of the story you create is entirely dependent on the quality of the prompts you feed into the AI.

ChatGPT is like a Formula One car—it's fast, powerful, and can do amazing things, but if you don't know how to drive it, you'll crash into the wall or just sit at the starting line spinning the wheels.

So, in this chapter, I want to give you a practical, ready-to-use collection of **excellent, proven prompt examples** specifically for thriller story design and structure. You'll be able to copy, adapt, and reuse these any time you want to speed up the writing process without losing quality or control.

Let's start with prompts for **story concept and idea generation.**

When you're at the very beginning and need an idea fast, try:

Prompt:

"Give me 10 original thriller story ideas that involve a missing person, a protagonist with a dark past, and a high-stakes conspiracy."

You can also narrow it down: **"Generate 5 psychological thriller plot concepts featuring unreliable narrators."**

"Create 3 techno-thriller story premises that revolve around cyber espionage."

These types of prompts give you a buffet of ideas quickly—and you can mix and match elements from different suggestions.

Once you've locked down an idea, you'll need to shape the **core conflict and structure.**

A great prompt for this is: **"Summarize the main conflict of this thriller story in one sentence."**

or

"Outline the three-act structure of a thriller story about [insert your idea]."

If you want more detail, go further: **"Break down the key plot points of this thriller in the three-act structure, including the inciting incident, midpoint twist, and climax."**

For character development, here are some killer prompts: **"Describe the protagonist's greatest fear and how it affects their decisions in this thriller."**

"Develop an antagonist who believes they're the hero of the story. What's their motivation and flaw?"

"List 5 personal stakes for the protagonist beyond life and death."

You can also get very specific: **"Create a character profile for a morally ambiguous private investigator protagonist, including flaw, secret, and internal conflict."**

If you want ChatGPT to help you with relationships and dynamics: **"Outline how the relationship between the protagonist and their closest ally evolves across the story."**

For pacing and structure, use prompts like: **"List cliffhanger chapter endings for this thriller story."**

"Suggest five ways to escalate tension in the second act of this thriller."

"Create a scene-by-scene outline for this thriller with increasing stakes and twists."

A fantastic use of ChatGPT is to help you stay focused while writing quickly. For example: **"What should happen in Chapter Three of this thriller to maintain tension and develop the plot?"**

When you want to brainstorm plot twists: **"Suggest three believable but unexpected twists for this thriller story."**

For subplot development: **"Create a subplot involving a supporting character that ties into the main thriller plot."**

You can also ask ChatGPT to help you control the balance between action and emotion: **"Suggest key moments where the protagonist's emotional arc should intersect with the thriller's main action."**

To tie your story together: **"List ways to foreshadow the final twist throughout this thriller story."**

When you're in the final stages of planning: **"Summarize the protagonist's character arc, the antagonist's plan, and the main plot twists in under 300 words."**

You can even ask for theme-based structural help: **"Outline how the theme of trust can be reflected in the plot structure of this thriller."**

And don't forget pacing: **"Create a timeline of events for this thriller story, showing how the tension escalates."**

The secret to these prompts is **specificity.**

The more detail you include about what you want, the better the results will be.

Avoid vague prompts like, "Write a thriller story" or "Give me a plot." Instead, give the AI clear boundaries and ingredients to work with.

If you ever feel stuck, use a diagnostic prompt like: **"Based on this outline, what's missing from the thriller's structure or character development?"**

You can even make ChatGPT your editor: **"Analyze this story outline and suggest how to improve the pacing and structure."**

One of the fastest ways to use prompts effectively is to create a **prompt chain.**

For example:

1. Generate a story idea.
2. Outline the three-act structure.
3. Develop character profiles.
4. Break down the key plot twists.
5. Map out scene-by-scene progression.

6. Brainstorm chapter cliffhangers.
7. Create emotional stakes and internal conflict.
8. Draft the first chapter.

Each step builds on the last—so you're writing fast but still keeping creative control.

When you combine all these prompt types, you can literally go from **zero to finished thriller outline in under an hour.**

And from there, writing the book itself becomes a process of filling in the blanks.

The key is learning how to drive ChatGPT like a creative partner, not a robot.

Your vision + strategic, well-structured prompts = thriller magic.

Examples of Good Prompts for Designing Compelling Characters

A great thriller lives or dies by its characters. Sure, readers come for the plot twists, the tension, the high-stakes action—but they stay because they're invested in the people caught up in the chaos. If your protagonist, antagonist, and supporting cast aren't compelling, no amount of shootouts, betrayals, or ticking clocks will save your story.

That's why one of the smartest ways to speed up your thriller writing is to learn how to use ChatGPT to help you **design rich, layered, believable characters—fast.** And the secret is simple: it's all in the prompts.

In this chapter, I'm going to give you a toolbox of clear, actionable prompt examples you can use whenever you need to create a thriller character quickly, without sacrificing depth or originality.

Let's start with your protagonist—the engine of your story.

If you're starting from scratch, try: **"Create a protagonist for a thriller story. They should be resourceful, morally conflicted, and haunted by a past mistake. Include their backstory, personality traits, flaw, and personal stakes."**

You can even make it more specific: **"Design a female journalist protagonist for a political thriller. She's driven, stubborn, but hiding a dangerous secret."**

"Create a protagonist who works as a cyber-security expert but is secretly being blackmailed."

Once you have the basics, you can go deeper: **"What is this protagonist's greatest fear, and how does it shape their decisions in the story?"**

"Describe a moment in this protagonist's past that still haunts them today."

For internal complexity: **"List three moral dilemmas the protagonist will face during the story."**

"What is the protagonist's biggest personal weakness that could sabotage them?"

You can also quickly generate emotional layers: **"Describe the protagonist's relationship with a close family member and how it influences their choices."**

Now, let's talk about your antagonist.

A one-dimensional villain isn't enough in a thriller. Readers want to understand the antagonist's motivation, even if they hate them.

Try prompting: **"Create a thriller antagonist who believes they are doing the right thing. Include their backstory, motivation, flaw, and relationship to the protagonist."**

Or: **"Design a psychologically complex antagonist for a thriller about corporate espionage. Include their personal code, secret weakness, and what they're willing to sacrifice to win."**

For added depth: **"Explain what childhood event shaped this antagonist's worldview."**

"List three reasons why readers might sympathize with this antagonist."

You can also use ChatGPT to generate **moral ambiguity: "Make the antagonist's motivation understandable but morally questionable."**

Once you've got your protagonist and antagonist, you'll want to fill in your supporting cast. These characters should do more than take up space—they should add tension, conflict, or emotional stakes.

Prompt ideas: **"Create three supporting characters for this thriller who each have a secret."**

"Design an ally character who is loyal to the protagonist but has their own hidden agenda."

"List five flaws or quirks for a supporting character who helps the protagonist but may betray them later."

For relationships: **"Describe the dynamic between the protagonist and their closest ally. How does it evolve over the story?"**

"Create a subplot involving a supporting character's personal conflict that intersects with the main thriller plot."

If you're writing a series, you can even plan future development: **"Outline how this supporting character could become the protagonist in a spin-off thriller."**

Another smart way to use ChatGPT is to make your characters feel more **real and grounded.**

Ask: **"List everyday habits, likes, and dislikes of this protagonist to make them more human."**

"Give this antagonist a harmless hobby that contrasts with their dark actions."

For internal tension: **"What lie does the protagonist believe about themselves at the start of the story?"**

"What secret is the antagonist hiding, even from their closest ally?"

And don't forget relationships between characters: **"List five ways the protagonist and antagonist mirror each other emotionally or psychologically."**

"Describe a complex relationship between the protagonist and a family member that adds emotional weight to the thriller."

If you want to turbocharge your character creation process, you can combine prompts: **"Create a protagonist, antagonist, and three supporting characters for a psychological thriller. Include each character's flaw, motivation, secret, and how they connect to each other."**

Then use ChatGPT to summarize: **"Summarize the character web for this thriller, showing the connections, conflicts, and alliances."**

And here's one of my favorite rapid-fire prompts: **"What's one thing the protagonist would never admit out loud?"**

"What's one thing the antagonist regrets but can't change?"

"What's one secret the supporting character is keeping from both the protagonist and antagonist?"

These small, sharp details can give your thriller characters that extra layer of realism that keeps readers hooked.

Finally, when you're writing at speed, it's easy to fall into cliché territory. So, once you've built your characters, ask ChatGPT to help you refine them: **"Analyze these characters and suggest ways to make them less stereotypical and more unique."**

By now, you should have a whole toolkit of character design prompts you can use over and over—whether you're writing your first thriller or your fifteenth.

Characters are the heart of every thriller.

And with the right prompts, you can create compelling, layered, unforgettable people in minutes, not months.

Examples of Good Prompts for World Building

When most writers think of world building, they imagine sprawling fantasy worlds or futuristic sci-fi landscapes. But here's the truth: **world building matters in thrillers too.**

It's not about creating imaginary kingdoms—it's about creating a setting that feels real, immersive, and charged with tension.

Whether your thriller is set in a dark alleyway in Prague, a corporate high-rise in New York, or a small town hiding deadly secrets, the world around your characters plays a huge role in shaping the mood, the stakes, and the reader's experience.

And when you're writing your thriller in one day, you don't have time to spend hours dreaming up every street corner and building blueprint. That's where **smart, focused ChatGPT prompts** come in.

In this chapter, I'll give you a toolbox of prompt examples you can use anytime you need to build your thriller's world quickly and effectively.

Let's start with the basics—**location.**

A thriller is only as strong as its setting.

To develop a dynamic setting fast, try:

Prompt:

"Describe a dark, atmospheric city setting for a modern thriller. Include key locations, landmarks, and the overall mood."

Or get more specific: **"Create a small-town setting for a psychological thriller. Include three places where secrets could be hidden."**

If you're writing an international thriller: **"Outline a globe-trotting thriller setting that moves between three countries. Include unique threats or obstacles in each location."**

Once you've got the geography, add some **local color: "Describe the sounds, smells, and atmosphere of a crowded night market where a chase scene could happen."**

"What unique, unsettling details can I include in a remote mountain village setting for a thriller?"

Your thriller setting should also reflect the **mood** of the story.

You can prompt: **"List five ways to make a city setting feel tense, oppressive, and dangerous."**

"Describe how to use weather and lighting to increase tension in a thriller scene."

A powerful world-building technique is to embed the **rules and culture** of the world into your story. Even if you're writing a contemporary thriller, your protagonist's world has its own codes and systems—whether it's the criminal underworld, the intelligence community, or the high-pressure world of finance.

You can prompt:

"Describe the unspoken rules and power dynamics of an international spy network."

"Outline how a corporate boardroom setting could be used as a dangerous, tense environment in a thriller."

"Create a believable criminal underground network in a modern city for a thriller story."

For **institutions** that shape the world: **"Describe a corrupt police department setting for a crime thriller."**

"Design a shadowy government agency for a political thriller. Include their public face and their secret operations."

If you want your thriller to involve surveillance, hacking, or espionage: **"List real-world surveillance technologies I can use in a techno-thriller setting."**

"Describe the hidden world of online criminal networks for a cyber-thriller."

Another layer of world building is the **social atmosphere.**

What's the public mood? Are people scared, angry, apathetic?

Prompt: **"Describe the social and political climate of a city on the brink of chaos in a thriller setting."**

You can also use world building to reflect the **theme** of your story: **"Suggest ways to make the setting of this thriller reinforce the theme of trust and betrayal."**

"Describe how the setting can mirror the protagonist's emotional state in a psychological thriller."

For practical details that ground your world: **"List five real locations in London where a high-stakes chase scene could take place."**

"Describe the layout and security features of a luxury penthouse used by a crime boss in a thriller."

When you want to build a world around **danger and secrets: "What are three places in a city where a secret meeting could take place without being noticed?"**

"Describe an abandoned building that could be used as a hideout in a thriller story."

For broader atmosphere: **"List five ways to make the setting of this thriller feel claustrophobic and tense."**

"Describe how to use a crowded public space to build suspense in a thriller scene."

If you're writing a series, you can even ask ChatGPT to help you plan a **recurring world: "Outline a consistent, recognizable setting that can be used across multiple books in a thriller series."**

Finally, remember that world building in thrillers isn't about creating elaborate lore—it's about creating a sense of place that enhances tension, danger, and immersion.

The more specific and sensory your world, the more your readers will feel like they're right there, racing alongside your protagonist, dodging danger at every turn.

Examples of Good Prompts for Ideas about the Thriller Scenarios

When it comes to writing thrillers, one of the fastest ways to speed up the process and get a powerful story rolling is knowing how to generate strong, gripping **scenarios.** The scenario is the engine of your thriller—it's the unique, high-stakes situation your characters are thrown into. It's the "what if" question that drives the entire plot.

And the good news is, you don't need to sit around for hours trying to come up with ideas. You can use ChatGPT to brainstorm brilliant thriller scenarios quickly—**if you know how to ask.**

That's what this chapter is all about: clear, effective, and creative prompt examples you can use anytime you need fresh, powerful ideas for your thriller storylines.

Let's start with the basics.

If you're at the very start and just need **raw thriller scenario ideas**, use prompts like: **"Give me 10 original thriller scenarios that involve betrayal, a missing person, and a ticking clock."**

"List 5 thriller story scenarios where an innocent person is framed for a crime they didn't commit."

"Suggest high-stakes thriller scenarios set in an isolated location like a cruise ship, a remote village, or an underground bunker."

You can also tailor prompts to the **sub-genre: "Create 3 political thriller scenarios involving government corruption and an assassination plot."**

"Suggest 5 psychological thriller scenarios where the protagonist can't trust their own memories."

"List cyber-thriller scenarios involving data theft and international espionage."

If you want to build something more **personal and character-driven**, prompt: **"Outline thriller scenarios where the protagonist's family member is in danger because of a secret from the past."**

"Suggest thriller story scenarios based on the protagonist's greatest fear coming true."

For fast brainstorming, you can request **scenario lists with specific hooks: "List 10 thriller scenarios with unexpected twists halfway through the story."**

"Give me 5 thriller scenario ideas where the antagonist is hiding in plain sight."

You can even ask for scenarios based on **location: "Suggest thriller scenarios that could take place entirely in a single night in New York City."**

"Create 3 small-town thriller scenarios involving buried secrets and old grudges."

When you're looking for **international or global stakes: "List 5 globe-trotting thriller scenarios where the protagonist is racing to stop a global disaster."**

"Give me international espionage thriller scenarios involving double agents and political intrigue."

If you want to explore **moral ambiguity** and tension, prompt: **"Suggest thriller scenarios where the protagonist has to choose between saving one person they love or thousands of strangers."**

"Create thriller scenarios where both the hero and the villain believe they're doing the right thing."

To make things even more unique, add an unusual twist: **"List thriller scenarios that combine a political conspiracy with a supernatural element."**

"Suggest thriller scenarios where the main character's biggest enemy is actually themselves."

If you're stuck and want ChatGPT to challenge you: **"Give me a thriller scenario idea that has never been done before."**

"Suggest a thriller scenario that flips the usual hero-villain dynamic."

You can also create **scenario formulas** and let ChatGPT fill in the blanks: **"Create a thriller scenario where a [Protagonist Role] is forced to [Action] when [Inciting Incident] happens in [Setting]."**

Example prompt: **"Create a thriller scenario where an investigative journalist is forced to clear their name when they're accused of espionage in Paris."**

For more specific character-driven scenarios: **"Outline a thriller scenario where a retired spy's child is kidnapped by one of their old enemies."**

"Describe a thriller scenario where the protagonist has 24 hours to solve a murder, but they're the prime suspect."

If you want something thematic: **"Give me thriller scenario ideas that explore the theme of trust and betrayal."**

"List thriller scenarios where the protagonist must uncover the truth but everyone around them is lying."

You can even use ChatGPT to give you **scene-level scenarios: "Describe a tense thriller scenario that could happen in a crowded airport."**

"Suggest a high-stakes confrontation scene scenario for a thriller climax."

For pacing and structure purposes: **"List escalating thriller scenarios for Act Two of a three-act thriller story."**

One of the best ways to use prompts is to chain them together.

Start with: **"Give me 5 thriller scenario ideas involving a whistleblower."**

Pick one you like, then ask:

"Outline the key plot points of this scenario."

Then follow up with:

"Suggest a protagonist, antagonist, and supporting cast for this scenario."

In less than an hour, you'll have a fully fleshed-out thriller premise ready to write.

The beauty of using prompts this way is that you can **control the direction.**

If an idea feels too cliché, ask: **"Make this scenario more original and unpredictable."**

Or if it feels too vague: **"Add specific details and a unique setting to this scenario."**

You can even use ChatGPT to help you combine ideas: **"Merge these two thriller scenarios into one compelling story."**

By learning how to ask the right questions, you can fill an entire notebook with thriller scenarios in a single afternoon—and you'll never stare at a blank page again.

You now have a powerful set of scenario prompts you can use any time you want to create fresh, exciting, tension-filled thrillers quickly and efficiently.

Your One-Day Thriller Writing Game Plan – From Start to Publish

You've made it. You've now learned every technique, every shortcut, and every trick to writing a gripping thriller in one day with ChatGPT as your creative partner. But before you close this book and dive into writing, you need one last thing—a clear, practical, step-by-step **game plan** you can follow from blank page to published book, all in a single day.

This chapter is your **one-day thriller writing blueprint.** Follow this process, and by the end of the day, you'll have a finished, formatted, published thriller ready for the world to read.

Step One: Story Concept and Structure (1-2 hours)

Start the day with your coffee, your laptop, and a clear head.

The first thing you'll do is **generate your thriller idea and structure.**

Use the prompts from earlier chapters to brainstorm a high-stakes scenario, a compelling protagonist and antagonist, and a simple three-act structure.

Quick prompts: **"Give me 5 original thriller story ideas involving betrayal and a race against time."**

"Outline the three-act structure of this thriller."

"Create character profiles for the protagonist, antagonist, and two supporting characters."

Once you've picked your idea, build a **scene-by-scene outline.**

Prompt: **"Break down this thriller plot into 15 short, high-tension scenes."**

This entire process should take no more than two hours.

Step Two: Write the First Draft (4-6 hours)

Once your outline is locked in, it's time to write.

Use ChatGPT to help you draft each scene based on your outline.

Prompt: **"Write Scene One of this thriller story. Keep it tense, fast-paced, and in an informal, engaging style."**

Do this scene by scene. Don't worry about perfection—your goal is to finish the draft.

Each scene should be around 800-1200 words.

If you're writing a 20,000-word novella, you'll want around 18-20 scenes.

If you're aiming for a shorter, punchy 10,000-word thriller, you can do 10-12 scenes.

You'll be surprised how fast you can move when you have the structure in place and ChatGPT filling in the heavy lifting.

Step Three: Quick Edit Pass (1-2 hours)

Once the draft is done, take a short break.

Then, read through the manuscript one chapter at a time.

Fix obvious typos, cut filler sentences, and tighten dialogue.

Use ChatGPT to speed up: **"Tighten this scene without losing tension."**

"Rewrite this dialogue to sound more natural and tense."

You're not looking for perfection. You're looking for a clean, sharp, readable draft.

Step Four: Write the Book Description and Front Matter (30 minutes)

Use prompts to generate your book description: **"Write a hook-heavy thriller book description based on this plot."**

Also write your front matter and author bio quickly: **"Write a short, engaging author bio for a thriller writer."**

Step Five: Format and Upload (1 hour)

Format your manuscript into a clean Word document.

Use clear headings, consistent font, and proper spacing.

You can also use a free formatting tool like **Reedsy Book Editor** or **Kindle Create.**

Create a basic book cover using **Canva, BookBrush, or KDP's Cover Creator.**

You already brainstormed cover ideas in Chapter 59, so you can execute one quickly.

Go to **kdp.amazon.com**, fill in your book details, upload your manuscript and cover, and hit **Publish.**

Your book will usually be live within hours.

Step Six: Announce and Market (30 minutes)

Once your book is published, use ChatGPT to help you write:

- A launch announcement email.
- A few social media posts.
- A short blog post about how you wrote a thriller in one day.

You can even ask: **"Write a promotional tweet announcing my new thriller eBook."**

And that's it.

In a single day, you've gone from blank page to finished, published thriller.

Your One-Day Thriller Checklist:

Story Idea and Outline

Character Profiles

Scene-by-Scene Draft

Quick Edit Pass

Book Description and Author Bio

Manuscript Formatting

Book Cover

Upload and Publish

Announce and Market

You'll notice that every step of the way, you're not starting from scratch.

You're using smart, specific prompts to keep the ideas flowing and the process moving fast.

Is it perfect? No.

But it's done.

And tomorrow, you can do it again. Or you can take what you've written, refine it further, and turn it into part of a series.

What matters is that you now know how to write, edit, publish, and market a complete thriller story **in a single day.**

You're no longer at the mercy of writer's block, overthinking, or perfectionism.

You're in control.

You're the storyteller.

And your next thriller is just one day away.

The Future of Writing Thrillers with AI

Now that you've made it through this entire book, learned how to write a thriller in one day, and discovered the power of structured prompting and creative control with ChatGPT, there's one last thing we need to talk about—**where all of this is heading.** Because the truth is, what you've learned here isn't just a trick for speeding up your writing. It's part of a much bigger shift happening in the world of storytelling.

We are living at the start of the age of **AI-assisted creativity.**

And whether you're excited about it or a little skeptical, one thing is certain: **the future of writing thrillers—and all fiction—is going to be powered by collaboration between humans and machines.**

Let's talk about what that future looks like, and what it means for you as a thriller writer.

First, let's clear something up.

AI isn't here to replace writers.

No AI tool can write a truly great thriller on its own, because thrillers aren't just about plot—they're about **emotion, tension, and human experience.**

What AI can do—and what you've been doing in this book—is act as a supercharged creative assistant.

It helps you brainstorm faster, organize your ideas better, and write more efficiently.

It's like having a writing partner who never runs out of energy, doesn't get stuck, and is ready to spit out 100 new plot twists at 2AM.

But this is just the beginning.

In the near future, AI will become even more personalized.

You'll be able to train your AI co-writer on your specific writing style, your voice, and your preferred pacing. Imagine having an AI that knows exactly how you like your characters to talk, how your action scenes flow, and what kind of twists you love to drop.

You'll be able to say: **"Write a thriller scene in my style, with a tension buildup like the one I used in Book Two, and a twist similar to Chapter 17 of my last novel."**

And it will do it.

AI tools will soon integrate directly into writing software, making it even faster and easier to go from idea to finished manuscript. You'll be able to brainstorm, draft, edit, format, and even publish—all inside one dashboard, powered by AI.

But it won't stop there.

AI will also change how we **research and fact-check** our thrillers.

Imagine being able to type: **"Give me accurate details about forensic investigation procedures in Chicago."**

Or: **"What's the current black-market price for a stolen passport in Eastern Europe?"**

And getting instant, reliable answers without wasting hours on Google rabbit holes.

You'll also see more integration of AI into **marketing and audience building.**

Instead of spending days writing newsletters, social media posts, and ad copy, you'll be able to generate an entire marketing campaign in minutes, tailored specifically to your thriller's themes, tone, and audience.

But here's where it gets even more interesting.

AI will soon help you **personalize stories for individual readers.**

You might be able to offer readers versions of your thriller where they can choose the ending, follow different character perspectives, or even insert themselves into the story.

Interactive, AI-assisted thrillers could become a whole new subgenre.

And as AI-generated images, trailers, and book covers become more sophisticated, you'll be able to create **complete multimedia storytelling experiences** around your thriller—all without needing a big publisher, a design team, or a massive budget.

That's the future.

But it's not without challenges.

As AI tools become more powerful and more people start using them, the market will get crowded.

There will be thousands of AI-assisted thrillers out there.

Many of them will be formulaic, rushed, or soulless—because their authors didn't learn how to control the process the way you have.

That's why the most important skill for the future isn't just knowing how to use AI—it's knowing how to stay in charge of the story.

Your creativity, your voice, your vision—that's what will make your thrillers stand out.

The future belongs to writers who know how to collaborate with AI without letting it take over.

Writers who can move fast, write smart, and stay true to their storytelling instincts while using the tech as a tool—not a crutch.

And the best part is—you're already ahead of the curve.

By learning how to use ChatGPT strategically, how to design your story structure, characters, world, and marketing plan, you've positioned yourself to thrive in this new era.

You can now write thrillers faster, sharper, and more consistently than most people ever imagined possible.

You're not at the mercy of writer's block, procrastination, or publishing gatekeepers.

You're in control.

And the future?

It's waiting for you to write it.

So, the next time someone says, "How is it possible to write a great thriller in one day?"

You'll smile, open your laptop, and show them exactly how it's done.

Because you don't just write thrillers.

You write the future of storytelling.

I hope you found inspiration within these pages. If you liked this book, please leave a review where you bought it. Thank you from the author.

www.ingramcontent.com/pod-product-compliance
Lightning Source LLC
LaVergne TN
LVHW082341200926
848481LV00012B/3411